CREATI

Loveplay

MW00452315

CREATIVE
Loveplay

SENSUAL WAYS TO EXPLORE
YOUR EROTIC FANTASIES

CARROLL & GRAF PUBLISHERS INC, NEW YORK

This edition first published in 1996 by
Carroll & Graf Publishers, Inc.
A Division of Avalon Publishing Group
19 West 21st Street
New York, New York 10010-6805

New edition 2001

©1996 Marshall Cavendish
©2001 Times Media Private Limitied

Produced by Marshall Cavendish Books
An imprint of Times Media Private Limited
A member of the Times Publishing Group
Times Centre, 1 New Industrial Road, Singapore 536196
Tel: (65) 2848844 Fax: (65) 2854871
E-mail: te@tpl.com.sg
Online bookstore: http://www.timesone.com.sg/te

All rights reserved

ISBN 0-7867-0881-6

Library of Congress Cataloging-in-Publication Data is available

Printed and bound in Italy

Contents

FOREWORD 6

Introduction

✤

CREATIVE LOVEPLAY is for couples who appreciate that lovemaking is a special part of their relationship and want to ensure that it is an exciting and erotic experience. A vibrant sexual relationship can be the key to a more intimate and trusting understanding of your partner, and this book reveals imaginative ways of making love which offer both partners greater rewards and fulfillment.

Sexual relationships frequently become a matter of routine, losing their original passion and scope as couples fail to experiment further with their bodies and desires. People often lack the knowledge to develop their lovemaking skills. As well as providing a variety of creative ideas for achieving a more erotic and imaginative sex life, this book is intended to encourage a couple to identify and communicate their needs and fantasies.

Sympathetically and clearly written, the subject is approached with the intention of making loveplay fun. You will find new ways of exploiting old positions and techniques, not forgetting the importance of foreplay and afterplay. There is a wealth of suggestions for ways of using aids, from food to feathers, to further stimulate the senses. Location is also an important aspect of lovemaking, and you will find that every room in your house can provide an appropriate backdrop for your sexual antics. For those who enjoy the fun of role play, there are many erotic scenarios to be tried. Together, these tips and suggestions will enable you to benefit fully from this unique aspect of your relationship.

Erotic Sex focuses on the wisdom and expertise of ancient sexual texts. Emphasis is placed on the unity of the couple, achieved through intimacy and an inexhaustible number of ways of making love.

Love Games shows you how to tantalize and tease your partner. Whether using a camera or a pack of cards, there is a variety of ideas on how to combine sex and games for the ultimate in sport.

Role Playing turns childhood games into adult fantasies with suggestions for different acts which will leave both partners unable to resist temptation.

Seductive Situations shows you how to make use of everyday locations and situations in your lovemaking. With a little imagination you can transform your relationship into a steamy, passionate affair.

1

Erotic Sex

The ancient civilizations of Arabia, India, Japan, and China recognized the importance of sexual pleasure and fulfillment. Writings on the subject are notable for their lack of restraint and the emphasis placed on the devotion and dedication required to achieve expert lovemaking. Follow their adventurous guidelines and you too can make your lovemaking an unforgettable experience.

A ARABIAN WAY OF LOVING

The sheikhs and concubines of antiquity learned their sexual skills with the help of a specially commissioned book. Uncover their secrets and find out what really happened during those mythical Arabian Nights.

▲ *It's easy to see why Nefzawi likens this position to a cavalier on horseback. The man has the option of leaning forward or sitting erect.*

*I*n the 16th century, at a time when the Arab civilization could rival any in the world in terms of culture and learning, a renowned scholar named Sheikh Umar ibn Muhammed al-Nefzawi was commissioned by his ruler, the Grand Vizir to the Bay of Tunis, to write a manual on the arts of love.

The result, entitled *The Perfumed Garden*, is among the most celebrated of all the eastern sex manuals, and contains a wealth of practical advice for the aspiring lover within its sensual, poetic pages.

MANUAL FOR MEN

The book is essentially an instruction manual for men on how to please women, and as such the roles of the two

a woman to climax simultaneously, and his instructions can therefore be seen as a way of redressing Nature's imbalance.

THE ELEVEN POSITIONS

The section of *The Perfumed Garden* dealing with intercourse is the most comprehensive of all the eastern sex manuals. It cites eleven classic Arab positions:

• The First Position. 'Make the woman lie upon her back, her thighs raised, then getting between her legs, introduce your member to her. Pressing your toes to the ground, you can move in her in a convenient, measured way.'

• The Second Position. 'If your member is short, let the woman lie on her back, lift her legs into the air so that they be as near her ears as possible, and in this posture, with her buttocks lifted up, her vulva will project forward.'

• The Third Position. 'Let the woman stretch herself upon the ground, and place yourself between her thighs. Then, putting one of her legs upon your shoulder and the other under your arm near the armpit, get into her.'

• The Fourth Position. 'Let her lie down, and put her legs on your shoulders. In this position, your member will

sexes are rigidly defined. True to the spirit of eastern sexual practice, Sheikh Nefzawi is at pains to stress the importance of foreplay as a preliminary to intercourse.

In doing so, he recognizes a phenomenon which research in the West has since confirmed – namely that, on average, a woman takes up to three times as long as a man to reach orgasm.

Nefzawi's ultimate aim is for a man and

▲▼ *The third and fourth positions are more variations on the missionary position where the pace and mood have increased and the degree of penetration is greater.*

WHAT'S IN A NAME?

THE FOLLOWING ARE JUST SOME OF THE COLORFUL NAMES GIVEN TO THE MALE AND FEMALE SEXUAL ORGANS IN *THE PERFUMED GARDEN*.

PENIS: EL HAMMAMA – THE PIGEON; EL TEUNNANA – THE TINKLER; EL ZODAMME – THE CROWBAR; EL KHORRATE – THE TURNABOUT.

VAGINA: ABOU KHOCHIME – THE ONE WITH A LITTLE NOSE; EL GUEUNFOND – THE HEDGEHOG; EL DEUKKAK – THE CRUSHER; EL NEUFFKAH – THE ONE THAT SWELLS; EL MOLKI – THE DUELLIST; EL SABEUR – THE RESIGNED.

◄ In this man-on-top position, the man raises the woman's leg and lifts her buttocks up towards him before he penetrates her.

just face her vulva, which must not touch the ground. And then introduce your member into her vagina.'

• The Fifth Position. 'Let her lie down on her side, they lay down yourself beside her on your side, and getting between her thighs put your member into her vagina.'

• The Sixth Position. 'Make her get down on her knees and elbows, as if kneeling in prayer. In this position the vulva is projected backwards. You then attack her from that side and put your member into her.'

• The Seventh Position. 'Place the woman on her side and squat between her thighs, with one of her legs on your shoulder and the other between your thighs, while she remains lying on her side. Then you enter her vagina and make her move by drawing her towards your chest.'

• The Eighth Position. 'Let her stretch herself on the ground, on her back with her legs crossed. Then mount her like a cavalier on horseback, being on your knees, while her legs are placed under her thighs.'

• The Ninth Position. 'Place the woman so that she leans with her front, or, if you prefer it, her back upon a low divan, with her feet set upon the ground. She thus offers her vulva to the introduction of your member.'

• The Tenth Position. 'Place the woman near to a low divan, the back of which she can take hold of with her hands. Then, getting under her, lift her legs to the height of your navel, and let her clasp you with her legs on each side of your body.'

• The Eleventh Position. 'Let her lie upon her back on the ground with a cushion under her posterior. Then, getting between her legs and letting her place the sole of her right foot against the sole of her left foot, introduce your member.' ♥

▼ In the Tenth Position the woman supports herself by gripping the end of the bed and clasps the man with her legs.

INDIAN WAY OF LOVING

Treat your partner to a night of exotic Indian lovemaking with the help of the greatest sex manual of all – the Kama Sutra.

Of all the ancient treatises on the art of love, the Indian *Kama Sutra* has had the greatest impact on western society. Thought to have been written between the first and fourth centuries AD, it is attributed to the sage Vatsyayana, who in turn quotes from the texts of several earlier scholars, believed to have received their wisdom directly from the Gods.

But popular misconceptions of the *Kama Sutra* abound. In reality, it is far from just a collection of ligament-straining positions, outdated customs and strange practices. On careful study it represents the cumulative experiences of a thousand years of sexuality, as practiced by one of the world's greatest civilizations. And like their counterparts, the Taoist pillow books, these manuals reveal an intuitive understanding of the joys and problems of lovemaking which time has not changed.

Only one section of the great tome is devoted to the technicalities of lovemaking; the others contain all the information young men or women of the time could wish to know.

The lovemaking section begins with advice on how to approach a lover, followed by instructions on kissing and foreplay, and then the positions and techniques for intercourse.

WHEN LOVERS MEET...

According to the *Kama Sutra*, when lovers meet, their bodies may touch lightly, rub against one another, 'pierce' each other (invade one another's 'personal space') or be pressed against a nearby solid object such as a wall.

From here, the encounter progresses to one of the four classic embraces. Standing, the couple may be entwined – The Twining of the Creeper – or else the woman may grip the man with one foot off the ground and the other on his foot – The Climbing of a Tree.

▲ *The Kiss. When one partner turns the face of the other by holding their chin and then kisses them, it is called a 'turned kiss.'*

◄ Woman playing the man. When her lover is fatigued, the woman should lay him on his back and give him assistance by acting his part.

Lying down on a bed, the lovers can entwine their limbs passionately around one another in The Mixture of Sesamum Seed with Rice. Or, the woman can sit on the man's lap in the embrace of Mixing Milk with Water.

The authors then mention variations in which the couple concentrate on close contact between their foreheads, breasts, and lower bodies. Implicit in the advice is that close bodily contact (as opposed to direct genital stimulation) is an essential preliminary to a satisfying bout of lovemaking.

KISSING WITH CONFIDENCE

While the authors of the *Kama Sutra* take care not to lay down a strict order for the various actions of lovemaking ('for love does not care for time or order'), they are at pains to stress the importance of correct and varied kissing. The forehead, eyes, cheeks, lips, throat, inside of the mouth and breasts are cited as the most kissable areas, although mention is also made of the arms, thighs and navel.

Kisses are classified both by intensity and according to the different roles

▼ Ending congress. After making love, the woman may lie in her partner's lap with her face towards the moon and he can show her the different stars.

played by the lips, tongue and teeth. As well as what is now known as the French kiss – appropriately called The Fighting of the Tongues – there are descriptions of more playful petting kisses in which one lip only is kissed, or where the tongue is held in reserve.

POSITIONS FOR LOVE

When it comes to intercourse itself, the *Kama Sutra* lays heavy emphasis on the various possible positions. The authors considered that these provided the variety necessary for a continually satisfying sex life, and saw them as a means of compensating for any incompatibility in size between the partners' sexual organs.

Most space is devoted to variations on the missionary position, with the man's action remaining the same, and the woman ringing most of the changes.

• The Widely Open position. Here the woman arches her back, lowers her head and stretches her legs apart.
• The Yawning position. She raises her thighs and keeps them wide apart.
• The Clasping position. The legs of both partners are stretched out and wrapped around one another.
• The Pressing position. This starts with

the Clasp, after which the woman squeezes the man with her thighs.

• The Mare's position. Here she holds his lingam (penis) inside her Yoni (vagina) while in a clasp.

• The Yawn. The woman places her legs on the man's shoulders.

• The Rise. She raises both legs straight up.

• The Press. She draws in her legs and presses them against his chest.

• The Half Press. Only one leg is drawn in this way against the man's chest.

• The Splitting of the Bamboo. Having adopted the Yawn, the woman stretches out first one leg then the other.

LOVEMAKING TECHINIQUES

The *Kama Sutra* states plainly that it is a man's duty to please a woman, and that this cannot be achieved successfully unless he gauges her disposition and then acts accordingly.

When the woman is ready, the man has the following options at his disposal:

• Moving forward – straightforward penetration of the yoni.

• Churning – holding and moving the lingam in the yoni.

• Pressing – pushing the lingam hard against the yoni.

HIGHS AND LOWS

A POINT OF SOME CONCERN TO THE AUTHORS OF THE *KAMA SUTRA* IS THAT THERE SHOULD BE COMPATIBILITY IN SIZE BETWEEN LOVERS' SEXUAL ORGANS. 'HIGH CONGRESS,' WHEN THE MAN'S LINGAM IS TOO LARGE FOR THE WOMAN'S YONI, AND 'LOW CONGRESS,' WHEN IT IS TOO SMALL, ARE BOTH CONSIDERED UNDESIRABLE. HOWEVER, THE AUTHORS SUGGEST THAT THE RIGHT CHOICE OF POSITION CAN GO SOME WAY TOWARDS REDRESSING THE BALANCE.

• Giving a Blow – removing the lingam from the yoni and striking the yoni with it.

• Piercing – penetrating from above and pushing against the clitoris.

• Blows of the Boar and Bull – rubbing the lingam against the sides of the yoni.

• Sporting of the Sparrow – moving the lingam rapidly in and out of the yoni.

When the woman takes the initiative she may also try:

• The Top – turning round on top of the lingam.

• The Pair of Tongs – grasping the lingam, drawing it into the yoni and squeezing it.

• The Swing – swaying from side to side. ❤

▲ *The embrace. Indicating the mutual love of a man and a woman, an embrace may be practiced at any time. It can be an act of tenderness after lovemaking or the first step towards rearousing your partner.*

CHINESE WAY OF LOVING

To the Ancient Chinese, sex was erotic, athletic, highly poetic and essential to the well-being of body and soul. So take a peek into the mores and methods of the past, and improve your sexual technique.

Three and a half thousand years before the so-called 'sexual revolution' there existed in China a civilization characterized, among other things, by a remarkably sophisticated attitude to sex.

This enlightened attitude sprung from Taoism – a part-religious part-philosophical movement which had established a firm foothold in Chinese cultural life by 2000 BC.

YIN AND YANG

To the Taoists, everything had an equal and opposite reaction. When something advances, something else must fall back. The forces responsible were given names – Yin, the passive, negative, nourishing force, and Yang, the consuming force.

When it came to human beings, the Taoists recognized the presence of both Yin and Yang. Men were thought to contain a large amount of Yang, while women had a higher proportion of Yin force, hence the names Lord Yang and Lady Yin used for male and female lovers.

The balance of Yin and Yang was always believed to be precarious. The way to correct this imbalance, according to Taoist belief, was for a man to take

▶ *Standing Bamboos:*
Lord Yang penetrates
Lady Yin's Golden Lotus
with his Coral Stem.

some of the woman's Yin force, and for her to take some of his Yang force – which could only be achieved by intercourse.

PILLOW BOOKS

Much of the accumulated wisdom of the Taoists was recorded in 'Pillow' books. These were as explicit in their many illustrations as they were comprehensive in their coverage of the subject. To western eyes, such books might easily be seen as pornographic. To the Chinese, however, they were simply recipes for living, to be consulted as frequently – and in much the same way – as a favorite cook book.

The language of the books may be flowery, but we can learn much from the Taoists' teaching and incorporate it into our lovemaking today.

THE CHINESE WAY

The oldest surviving sex manual was written by Huang-Ti, The Yellow Emperor, about 2500 years BC. It was written in the form of questions and answers. When the Yellow Emperor inquired of his goddess-instructress, the Wise Maiden, as to how the right mood for love could be induced, she advised

▲ *The Tiger in the Forest: Lady Yin kneels down and lowers her head. Lord Yang inserts his Swelling Mushroom into the Vermilion Gate.*

▼ *Cicadas Mating: Lady Yin lies face down with her Golden Gully pointing upwards. Lord Yang buries his Coral Stem deep inside her Receptive Vase.*

him to follow the 'Five Natural Humors of the Male.'

The first 'natural humor' was to be relaxed and unassuming, the second to be generous of spirit, the third to be controlled in breathing and the fourth to be serene in body. The fifth humor – a desire for solitude brought on by feelings of loyalty – was the only legitimate excuse a man could give for the failure of his Jade Stem to stiffen.

The Wise Maiden proceeded to

THE LANGUAGE OF LOVE

INTERCOURSE: THE CLOUDS AND THE RAIN; THE MISTS IN THE RAIN; THE MOUNTAIN OF WU.
ORGASM: BURSTING OF THE CLOUDS; THE GREAT TYPHOON.
MALE SEXUAL ORGAN: MALE PEAK, STALK OR STEM, JADE STEM, CORAL STEM; RED BIRD; SWELLING MUSHROOM.
FEMALE SEXUAL ORGANS: JADE GATE OR PAVILION; OPEN PEONY BLOSSOM; GOLDEN LOTUS; CORAL GATE; PEARL ON THE JADE STEP (CLITORIS); GOLDEN GULLY (LABIAL CLEFT); THE JEWEL TERRACE.

advise The Yellow Emperor to be guided by the Five Responses of the Female. First, when she became flushed, the man should approach her. Then, as her nipples rose and beads of perspiration appeared on her nose, he would know his advances were welcome.

The next stage in the Chinese sexual act was foreplay. This held great importance for the Taoist Masters, who believed that only if the Yin and Yang forces were stirred slowly into action could they reach full potency.

In the case of a new or inexperienced partner, Master Tung Hsuan (believed to be a 7th-century physician) counseled tenderness, consideration and restrained exploration, accompanied by soft caresses, reassuring words and gentle kisses.

INTIMATE TOUCHING

After these initial embraces came more intimate touching, with the woman fondling the man's Jade Stem and causing her own Yin essence to flow.

But even though by now both partners could be thought ready to unite, Tung Hsuan advised 'further dalliance' before penetration was attempted.

The man should allow his Jade Stem

▲ *The Swinging Monkey: Lady Yin lowers herself on to Lord Yang's lap. She slides her Jewel Terrace over his Red Bird.*

▼ *The Dragon in Flight: Lady Yin lies on her back with her legs raised. Lord Yang parts her feet and lowers his Jade Stem into her Golden Pavilion.*

(penis) to hover over the Cinnabar Gate (vagina) while kissing the woman lovingly and gazing down at her Golden Gully. He should stroke her breasts and stomach while allowing his Male Peak to flick the sides of the Examination Hall (labia) and caress the Jewel Terrace (clitoral area). And if necessary, he should kiss and lick the Pearl on the Jade Step (clitoris) to ensure that the Yin essences were thoroughly stirred before the Clouds and the Rain (intercourse).

As the Jade Pavilion reached full lubrication, so the man should plunge ever deeper, slanting to the left and right, sweeping in a circular motion, and alternating deep thrusts with shallow strokes.

BASIC POSITIONS

Although fundamental Taoist beliefs suggested that it was preferable for Lord Yang always to mount Lady Yin from above, and despite the fact that variations on the missionary position remained the most popular, the Taoist masters never hesitated to extol the virtues of adopting more adventurous poses during lovemaking. ❤

JAPANESE WAY OF LOVE

The ancient Japanese seized their sexual pleasure with passion and enthusiasm. Take your inspiration from their wonderfully erotic antique prints and make love with your partner eastern style.

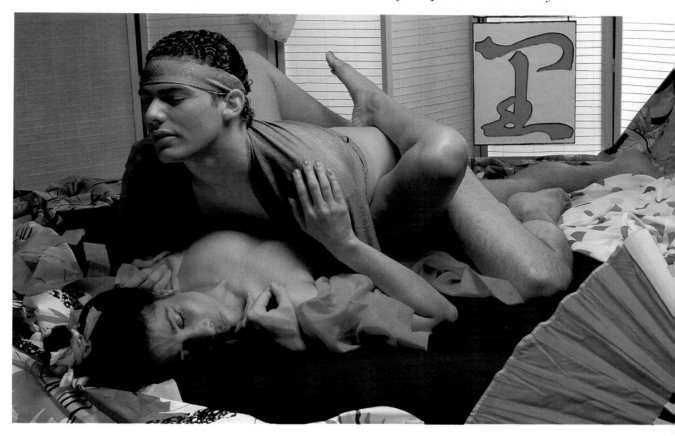

▲ *The ancient Japanese believed that sexual pleasure provided its own rewards. They wrote about the most erotic sexual techniques with wit and imagination, but without a hint of shame. We can learn a great deal from them today.*

Like many ancient cultures, the Japanese have a rich and enviable sexual heritage, much of which is surrounded, even today, with exoticism and mystery.

A large portion of its poetry, literature and art was devoted to the finer skills of lovemaking, and the paintings and illustrations that have survived, together with the texts so far translated, are masterpieces of sensuality.

The most explicitly erotic of the many prints, scrolls and book illustrations are called shunga, or 'spring drawings'.

SHUNGA SEXUALITY

There are many remarkable features about shunga prints, but two are striking on first glance. First, the lovers are rarely naked. This could hardly be put down to prudishness given the content of the pictures. The Japanese simply

provided the materials. Sex aids were freely available – there were dildos of every shape, size and material, including beautiful and very expensive tortoise-shell examples for the most discriminating noblewoman.

Double dildos were a great favourite among the ladies of the court, whose movements in the outside world were restricted to one excursion every six months. Hollow metal spheres that contained one or more metal balls were also popular – lodged in the vagina, they vibrated pleasingly on the slightest movement.

For men there were outsize hollow penises (perhaps for those who felt a little inadequate by shunga standards!). There were also rings with small buttons attached which increased friction.

thought that sensuous, loose-fitting clothing heightened sexual attraction.

Secondly, the sexual organs in all the pictures are grossly exaggerated – the vulvas gaping wide and often dripping, the pubic hair luxuriant, the penises massively swollen, heavily veined and bristling with hair. The reason for this is that the artist wanted to emphasize the sexual act itself, rather than the participants as individuals.

NO RESTRAINT

The subject matter of the prints makes clear the completely unrestrained Japanese approach to sex. There are often two or more women making love to one man, or to each other. Everything was natural to the ancient Japanese.

Women are frequently observed masturbating with a dildo, lying or sitting back with the dildo strapped to a foot. Dreams and fantasies, sometimes involving sex with animals or mythical creatures, are freely portrayed.

SEX AIDS

Once the prints and texts had provided the inspiration, the sex shops of the day

▲ *The resin oozes from the pines. The man enters the woman from behind and can caress her at his leisure.*

▼ *Enter the deep waters. Rear entry allows the man total control over lovemaking.*

THE SEXUAL ACT

The shunga prints present the sexual act in an almost inexhaustible variety of ways. One classic book illustrates the 48 positions considered practicable or possible for heterosexual couples to enjoy.

Naturally, many of these positions are

only minor variations on others, but they indicate the ingenuity of a people who were eager to explore the very furthest shores of their sexual capacity with their partners.

FOCUS ON FOREPLAY

While the ancient Japanese described a whole variety of sexual techniques, they paid particular attention to the importance and value of foreplay:

*'Knowledgeable gardeners always begin
By watering the spring grass.'*

A man who holds the secrets of arousing

▲ All can be done to another with lip service. A woman performing oral sex is considered the supreme love-gift.

▼ All her mouths attract kisses. The man uses his tongue, leaving his hands free to explore her body.

his partner will ultimately reap the rewards for himself:

*'If you know how to approach her,
She will mix every night
Her honey with your milk.'*

The Japanese recognized oral sex as a means of foreplay and an end in itself:

*'Everything can be done with lip service,
Even love.'*

The descriptions and advice are appropriate, but the language lends cunnilingus a charm all of its own:

*'If the cup is deep
Plunge your tongue into it several times.'*

Fellatio was written about with undisguised gusto:

*'If she sucks the grains of rice
Of which your sake is made,
It will only be the better for it.'*

The Japanese lover also recognized the value of afterplay, even if only as a means of ensuring his own pleasure later on:

*'Sowing seed is nothing if one neglects
The garden thereafter.'*

Much can be learned from the Japanese delight in sexual matters, and a brief foray into the mystic east with your partner could yield wonderful rewards. ❤

WHY NOT...

PREPARE A SPECIAL TREAT FOR YOUR PARTNER – A NIGHT OF PASSIONATE JAPANESE-STYLE LOVEMAKING ON A THICK RUG PLACED ON THE FLOOR

HAVE A GLASS OF WARMED SAKE (RICE WINE) BEFORE SEX AS AN APHRODISIAC

MAKE LOVE IN A SILKEN KIMONO TO GIVE YOUR LOVER JUST A TANTALIZING GLIMPSE OF YOUR BODY

WEAVE A JAPANESE SEXUAL FANTASY, WITH THE SCENT OF CHERRY BLOSSOM, GEISHA GIRLS AND SAMURAI WARRIORS

*A*DVANCED ARABIAN LOVEMAKING

Sexual excitement may fluctuate in even the most loving relationship. Fantasy can help to brighten up any dull moments that partners may experience.

*E*xpert lovemaking requires devotion and dedication. To those who practice the art, the Arabian masters offer a unique variety.

The Arabian philosophy on intercourse was that it should be frequent, prolonged and culminate in orgasm for both partners. This was based on two precepts – that the ecstasy of orgasm symbolized union with God, and that an imaginative and varied sex life keeps husband and wife together in happiness. Sheik Nefzawi, author of the celebrated manual, *The Perfumed Garden*, believed that every 'act of combat' should end in orgasm for both partners, and, in his extensive descriptions of lovemaking positions, he attempted to link the positions to the needs and physical characteristics of the lovers.

THE BEST POSITIONS

Of the 25 positions he derived from his readings of Indian scripts Nefzawi stated that 'the majority of them do not yield enjoyment, and give more pain than pleasure!'.

But he acknowledged that the Indians had 'advanced further than we in the knowledge of the investigation of the coitus and that all the positions should be tried.'

POSITIONS TO TRY

Here are a selection of some of the more popular positions he recommended.

▲ *Legs in the air. She lies with her legs up against her partner's shoulders and closes her thighs around his penis, to allow a tighter grip.*

• Pounding on the spot. The man sits down with his legs stretched out. The woman then sits astride his thighs, supporting herself on her hands, crossing her legs behind the man's back. She positions the entrance to her vagina opposite his penis and guides it into the entrance. She now places her arms around his neck and he holds her sides and waist, helping her to rise and fall upon his penis.

• The screw of Archimedes. The man

woman's feet should rest upon a cushion to enable her to keep her vulva in concordance with his member.'
• The race of the member. The man lies on his back with cushions raising his shoulders, but with his buttocks firmly on the bed. He draws up his legs until his knees are level with his face. The woman now sits down on to his penis. Strict advice to the woman is 'she must not lie down, but keep seated as if on horseback – the saddle being the knees and the stomach of the man.' In that position she can, by the play of her knees, work up and down.

MAN-ON-TOP POSITIONS
• The stopperage. As this position can be painful for the woman, Nefzawi only recommends it if the man's member is short or 'soft.' Place the woman on her back with a cushion under her buttocks. The man kneels between her legs and bends her thighs against her chest as far as possible. The man can now place his penis in her vagina. At the moment of ejaculation the man should draw the woman towards himself.
• Frog fashion. The woman lies on her

lies stretched out on his back. The woman sits on his penis, facing him, and holds herself upon her hands to make sure that her stomach does not touch his. The movement of the woman is up and down, and, if the man is fit, he can assist her from below.
• The double view of posteriors. The man lies stretched out on his back, and the woman sits down on his penis, facing away from him. The man presses her sides between his thighs and legs while she supports herself on the bed with her hands as she rises and falls on the penis. The position is so called because if the woman 'lowers her head, her eyes are turned towards the buttocks of the man.'
• Interchange in lovemaking. This is an active position for the woman, the basic idea being that the woman fulfils the traditional part of the man and the man is passive like a woman.
   The man lies on his back and the woman kneels between his thighs. She lifts his buttocks until his erect penis is opposite her vagina, and then guides the penis inside her with her hands. 'The

▲ *Pounding on the spot. Use this position to control the depth of penetration and the pace of lovemaking.*

▼ *Frog fashion. For comfort, the woman lies on her back with the man sitting close to her.*

DIFFERING SHAPES AND SIZES

SHEIK NEFZAWI HAD ADVICE FOR PARTNERS OF DIFFERENT SIZES.

• THE WOMAN LIES ON HER BACK WITH A THICK CUSHION UNDER HER BUTTOCKS, AND UNDER HER HEAD. SHE THEN DRAWS UP HER THIGHS TO HER CHEST. THE MAN LIES ON HER, INTRODUCES HIS PENIS, TAKES HOLD OF HER SHOULDERS AND DRAWS HIMSELF UP TOWARDS THEM.

• BOTH THE MAN AND WOMAN LIE FACE TO FACE ON THEIR SIDES. THE WOMAN SLIDES HER UNDERMOST THIGH UNDER THE MAN'S SIDE AND PUTS THE OTHER ONE OVER HIS. THEN SHE ARCHES HER STOMACH OUT, WHILE HIS PENIS IS PENETRATING HER VAGINA. BOTH HOLD EACH OTHER'S NECK AND THE WOMAN CROSSES HER LEGS OVER HIS BACK AND DRAWS HIM IN CLOSE.

• THE MAN LIES ON HIS BACK WITH HIS LEGS STRETCHED OUT. THE WOMAN SITS ON HIS PENIS AND, STRETCHING HERSELF DOWN OVER HIM, SHE PULLS HER KNEES UP TO THE HEIGHT OF HER STOMACH. HOLDING HIS SHOULDERS, SHE PRESSES HER LIPS TO HIS.

back and pulls her legs back until her heels touch her thighs. The man sits close to her with his penis opposite the entrance to her vagina. When his penis is inserted, the man places the woman's knees under his armpits and holds her upper arms to draw her towards him at the moment of orgasm.

• The toes cramped. The woman lies on her back with the man kneeling between her thighs. The man lifts the woman's buttocks so that she can cross her legs over his back. He then lifts her so she can get her arms around his neck.

• Legs in the air. In this position the woman keeps her thighs closed, thus 'making a tighter comfort for any man's member.' The woman lies on her back and the man raises her legs until they are vertical. The man continues to hold up the woman's legs while he encircles her with his thighs and places his penis in her vagina.

• The tail of the ostrich. The woman lies on her back and the man kneels in front of her. He lifts up her legs until only her head and shoulders remain in contact with the bed. He enters her vagina and holds on to her buttocks.

▼ *The double view of posteriors allows the man to look at and caress his partner's bottom while she rises and falls on his penis.*

Movement is created by his pushing and pulling on her buttocks.

• The seducer. The woman lies on her back and the man sits on his legs between her legs. He lifts her up and separates her thighs and places her legs under his arms. He then holds her waist or shoulders and pulls her on to his penis. He then pushes back and forth.

EASIER POSITIONS

Both the following positions require less exertion than others mentioned but they can still give an enjoyable and imaginative angle to your lovemaking.

• The manner of the bull. The woman lies on her stomach, her buttocks raised by cushions. The man approaches from behind, stretches along her back and inserts his penis. Nefzawi concludes that 'this is the easiest of all methods.'

• Driving the peg home. The woman holds the man's neck, clasps his waist with her thighs and steadies herself by leaning against a wall. Then 'thus suspended, the man insinuates his pin into her vulva.' ❤

ADVANCED INDIAN LOVEMAKING

The Ancient Indians considered foreplay as important as the sexual act itself, and much of the advice in the great manuals of the time is just as fresh and relevant to lovers today as it was in antiquity.

The ancient Indian sex manuals make no secret of the fact that sex is not something you learn overnight. The authors of the celebrated *Kama Sutra, Ananga Ranga* and the *Khoka Shastra* were well aware that lovemaking embraces almost all aspects of human existence from what you eat to the way you decorate your bedroom – and that only by taking such things into account can anyone hope to become a master of the art.

Rather than rushing headlong into lovemaking, the manuals advise that the man should take his time in becoming intimate with his partner, beginning with the slowest, gentlest caresses, kneeling all the while at his lover's feet so that at no time does she feel threatened.

KISSES FOR FOREPLAY

One of the great Indian love manuals, the *Ananga Ranga*, recommends that certain kisses should accompany this early phase of foreplay.

In the *Ghatika*, or 'neck-nape' kiss, the woman covers her lover's eyes with her hands and then, closing her own eyes, thrusts her tongue into his mouth

▶ *Embracing was considered to be one of the most important elements of foreplay.*

in a series of deep, slow, rhythmic movements which are a parody of the act of intercourse itself.

In the *Uttaroshtha*, or 'upper-lip' kiss, she takes his lower lip between her teeth then chews and bites it gently. He, meanwhile, does the same with her upper lip.

In the *Pratibodha*, or 'awakening' kiss, one of the couple, on finding the other fast asleep, presses their lips to them and gradually increases the pressure until they wake.

THE POWER OF FINGERNAILS

The ancient sex counselors of India were firm believers in the power of the fingernails to titillate and arouse during foreplay. Pages of the manuals are devoted to describing how – and even when – lovers' nails may be used to best effect.

Light, dabbing movements on the breasts, back, buttocks and thighs are designed to produce a delicious shuddering sensation in the recipient.

▶ *Woman-on-top positions were practiced and perfected by some of India's most celebrated courtesans. In the 'Contrary Position' the man lies outstretched on his back and his lover lies on top, flat on her stomach. Once he has entered her, she then arches her back, presses her hands into his waist, and uses these as leverage to swing her hips in a circular motion.*

▼ *A variation of an Indian standing position – if the man kneels down, his partner can easily wrap one leg around his waist as he penetrates her. Kneeling makes this position less tiring.*

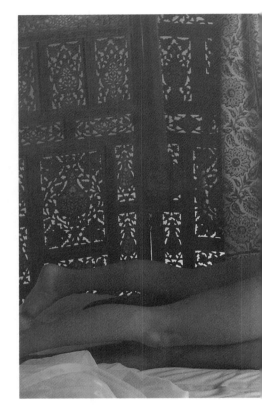

Anything deeper, warns the *Ananga Ranga*, must be used with caution at the heights of passion – and then only with the recipient's full consent.

LOVING BITES AND HAIR PULLING

Much the same goes for biting, another foreplay technique favored by the Indians, although in this case, the lips, cheeks, neck and breasts come in for the most attention. And here too, there is a strict code of practice to stop things getting out of hand. Where a man is doing the biting, the authors state that when the woman utters a sharp, high-pitched sound, he should take it as a sign to stop.

The most favored bite of all, and one said to require 'great practice' to perfect, is the *Pravalamani-dashana*, or 'coral bite,' – a protracted and passionate union of a man's teeth and a woman's

lips, in which sucking, nibbling and nipping all play their part.

Alone among the ancient civilizations, the Indians exhibit a great fascination for hair, and the *Ananga Ranga* lists four ways in which the erotic possibilities of this much neglected part of the body might be explored.

First, the man may clasp his lover's hair. From here, he can then draw her towards him, sliding his hands around behind her head. As passions mount, the man should grasp a knot of her hair tightly while embracing her. Then as the couple come together, they can run their fingers through each other's hair, ruffling and pulling it as they do so before moving on to lovemaking.

TOWARDS PERFECT HARMONY

Like modern-day counselors, the authors of the Indian sex manuals realized that there is no greater threat to a happy sexual relationship than boredom and predictability.

While they all assume that an inexperienced couple is likely to spend most of their time trying out variations of the classic missionary position, the *Ananga Ranga* in particular goes on to describe others – sitting, standing rear-entry and woman-on-top – so that more jaded palates might continue to have something to excite them.   ❤

◀ *'In the Manner of the Bull' is a rear-entry position suggested in the* Ananga Ranga. *The woman kneels on all fours while her partner enters her from behind.*

WHAT EVERY MAN SHOULD KNOW

THE *KAMA SUTRA* CONTAINS PLENTY OF USEFUL HINTS FOR THE MODERN MAN-ABOUT-TOWN, INCLUDING SUGGESTIONS ON HOW TO DECORATE HIS BEDROOM FOR NIGHTS OF LOVE. AS WELL AS A BED – SOFT AND COVERED WITH A CLEAN WHITE CLOTH, PLUS GARLANDS AND BUNCHES OF FLOWERS – HE IS ADVISED TO INVEST IN ANOTHER COUCH, WITH A STOOL AT THE HEAD UPON WHICH TO PLACE THE 'FRAGRANT OINTMENTS OF THE NIGHT.' OTHER ESSENTIALS INCLUDE A POT FOR SPITTING, A BOX CONTAINING ORNAMENTS, A LUTE HANGING FROM A PEG MADE OF AN ELEPHANT'S TOOTH, A DRAWING BOARD, A POT OF PERFUME, SOME BOOKS, A BOARD FOR PLAYING DICE AND, BY THE DOOR, A BIRDCAGE!

*A*DVANCED CHINESE LOVEMAKING

The ancient Chinese masters considered that lovemaking should be a unique experience – every time. Their techniques allowed for almost every conceivable variation.

To the Taoist philosophers who shaped the attitudes of the ancient Chinese, sex was not something to be hurried or whispered about behind closed doors. It was an art – to be studied, practiced and perfected. There is much to be learned from this relaxed and liberated view of lovemaking.

THE PLEASURE PRINCIPLE

The essence of the Taoist attitude toward sex, as stated in the celebrated pillow books (historic sex manuals), was that making love stimulates the flow of the life-giving Yin and Yang energies between men and women. This in turn made it a highly desirable occupation, and one that people were encouraged to engage in whenever – and wherever – possible.

The basic pillow book advice on lovemaking contains a wealth of material on how to set the scene for love, how to make love to please a woman, and how a man can control himself until his partner has herself experienced a climax.

▶ *Taoist philosophy holds that both partners must be truly satisfied for the Yin and Yang energy flow between the man and the woman to have any benefit.*

The recipe for sexual success is to combine practice – from which grows increased confidence and technique – with experimentation, to keep the flames of passion burning. The pillow book conclusions are really no different from those of contemporary sex therapists – namely that an exciting sexual relationship has to be worked at by both partners.

MAKING ADVANCES

Retiring to the bedchamber in the wrong mood is the most common form of impotence. This advice, given by the Wise Maiden to the Emperor Won Hung Lo more than 5000 years ago, is as worthy of note today as it was then. If either partner feels uncomfortable, neither will be in the mood for relaxed lovemaking.

▲ *'Lord Yang gently teases Lady Yin awake with a thousand soft kisses.'*

Pillow books suggest setting the scene with care. In ancient China erotic wallhangings, subdued lights and scented sheets were employed to create a romantic atmosphere, thereby stimulating the occupants' desire to make love.

HOW TO CHOOSE A WOMAN

NOT DISSIMILAR TO MOST MEN THROUGHOUT HISTORY, THE ANCIENT TAOIST MASTERS BELIEVED THEY COULD JUDGE A WOMAN'S SEXUAL PERSONA FROM HER PHYSICAL CHARACTERISTICS. THE FOLLOWING TIPS WERE GIVEN BY MASTER TE-HUI, IN A PIECE CALLED *HOW TO CHOOSE A WOMAN*.

IF HER BUTTOCKS ARE:

• HIGH AND PROTRUDING – DEMANDING AND HARD TO SATISFY;
• FLAT – SHE SHOULD LABOR IN THE KITCHEN;
• NARROW – SHE WILL SELDOM HAVE ORGASMS;
• DROOPING – SHE WILL BE LAZY AND PASSIVE.

In a modern context, this means thinking about simple touches like subtle lighting, plenty of pillows or perhaps glossy satin sheets – all of which can transform a bedroom into a warm inviting love nest.

▲ *Taoist masters do not consider that it is technique alone that makes for a fabulous sex life.*

Soothing background music helps too, and with a modern hi-fi you can go one better than the wealthy lovers of the Orient, who frequently had a maidservant stand nearby reciting poetry while they made love.

BREAKING DOWN BARRIERS
While never underestimating the power of surroundings, the Taoist masters were too clever to assume that this alone would launch couples into abandoned lovemaking.

In their teachings they accept that one or even both partners might feel hesitant or inhibited. To overcome this they suggest that couples, before even touching each other, place a pillow book on the bed and look through it together. This way, the more hesitant partner – in ancient China, it would probably be a shy young bride – can become aroused without too much performance pressure.

◀ *'Like a tiger from the forest, Lord Yang leaps upon Lady Yin, pushing his Iron Implement into the Coral Gate.'*

The masters continue, pointing out that if the less inhibited partner is at all sensitive, they will quickly realize which images and stories appeal to their lover, and will then feel encouraged to begin caressing them.

Thus, by Taoist reckoning, there is nothing strange in the fact that many couples today use erotic books, magazines and videos to help get them in the mood. Nor would they question the fact that reading or watching erotic material makes it easier for lovers to say what turns them on.

TOUCH SENSITIVE

The pillow books recommend that a couple move on from this stage of subtle excitement of the senses to more direct stimulation only when they have both let each other know they are fully aroused.

Accepting that women frequently take longer than men to reach a state

▲ *'Lady Yin opens her golden Lotus, captures Lord Yang's Heavenly Dragon Pillar and falls and rises until the coming of the Great Typhoon.'*

◄ *'Her Golden Gulley hovers over his Red Bird. He butts her fiercely until they both find the Bursting of the Clouds.'*

of readiness for intercourse, the pillow books stress that it is a man's duty to take the lead in a session of foreplay.

Starting with general caresses and the whispering of sweet words, a man is then advised to move on to kissing the breasts and the Jade Step (clitoris) until the time is right to begin his assault on the Jade Pavillion (vagina).

THE ACT OF LOVE

Since sustained pleasure and climax are the ultimate goals of Taoist teaching, it is hardly surprising that pillow books contain a wealth of instruction on different positions for love. Ranging from common sense to downright hazardous, their purpose is to keep the flame of desire burning.

Taoist sexual teaching can have many benefits. When a couple set out together to explore each other's bodies in a playful and relaxed way, the pressure to 'perform' is removed and both partners can let their senses take over. Isn't it worth considering converting to sexual abandon? ♥

2

Love Games

M aking love should not become merely a repetitive exercise. What better way to vary your sexual routine than to make a game of it, with high stakes, winners and losers, and the ultimate of prizes? The following suggestions will help you to lose any inhibitions you might have about experimenting with different ideas for foreplay, and with your body. While enjoying the stimulation, you can slowly reach a climax to your actions.

PLAYING CARDS

Take a pack of cards, dim the lights, and let the excitement mount as you challenge your partner to an unforgettable game of skill and chance where there are no losers.

A good game of cards can be as exciting as a night of passion. The freshness of a crisp new pack, the shuffle and the deal, the rush of adrenalin as you pit your wits against your opponent, and the skill with which you play your hand, make the pastime a singularly erotic event.

Few of us ever have the chance to gamble for high stakes, and the gaming tables of top casinos remain the preserve of James Bond movies. But you can, in the privacy of your own home, risk losing your body to your partner for one wild night of cards and love.

The most famous of all erotic games is the traditional strip poker. This can be played using any form of the poker game, in which you bluff your opponent into thinking that the five-card hand you hold is the highest around the table.

However, the object is always the same – the loser in each round has to remove an article of clothing, while the winner is the one who manages to retain their modesty the longest.

The thrill of the game is the ultimate aphrodisiac, as each hand played brings you closer to what is to come. Make yourselves warm and comfortable, unplug the telephone and have a drink close at hand.

It is a good idea to set a few rules before you begin. Decide what does and does not count as clothing – items such as rings and watches for instance – otherwise you could find yourself in your underwear before your opponent

▼ *The risk element in strip poker, where both partners have to peel off their clothes bit by bit, can act as a tantalizing prelude to sex.*

have to take some – or all – of them off with as much grace and style as you can. Don't choose difficult or unsexy items such as turtleneck sweaters or jogging bottoms – neither will look especially attractive when you wriggle out of them.

For him, choose boxer shorts, button fly jeans and a front-fastening shirt. For her, start with the right underwear and layer the clothes on top. Choose a basque or bra and panties rather than a teddy – teddies may look attractive but they are difficult to remove with style. Stockings with a suspender belt are a better choice than tights, and they count as three items, not one! Finish with an easily removable blouse together with a skirt or button-fly jeans. When you are both comfortable, you can let the fun and games begin!

FORFEITS AND FAVORS

Once you have succeeded in gambling all the clothes from your partner's body (or lost all of your own), the game usually comes to a riotous close. But why not prolong the anticipation and play on for forfeits and favors? This time the loser, as they can no longer remove any clothing, has to perform an act dictated

▲▼ Playing for forfeits and favors adds extra spice to your card game. The loser has to carry out any task dictated by the winner – this might be a simple but sensuous massage or any new and erotic form of foreplay that you have always fantasized about, but never dared perform!

starts on their other garments!

If your partner doesn't spring the idea of a game on you as a surprise, you will have time to prepare yourself in advance for a sensuous night. Start with a scented bath or refreshing shower, then cover your skin with perfumed body cream or splash on some aftershave.

The most important part of the preparation is the clothes you choose to wear. Select them carefully as you will

DOS AND DON'TS

DO SET RULES BEFORE YOU BEGIN. OTHERWISE YOU COULD FIND YOURSELF UNDRESSED WAY BEFORE YOUR PARTNER.

DO DECIDE AT WHICH POINT YOU ARE GOING TO FINISH THE GAME – WITH, FOR EXAMPLE, THE FIRST OR SECOND FORFEIT.

DON'T INSIST ON CONTINUING THE GAME IF YOUR PARTNER WANTS TO STOP.

DON'T WRITE DOWN A FAVOR THAT YOU KNOW YOUR PARTNER WOULD BE UNHAPPY PERFORMING.

by the winner, the cards enabling you to enjoy a new kind of foreplay.

You can be as chaste as you like – a kiss on the cheek, a stroke of the thigh – and work up to more exciting favors until the game becomes a secondary consideration.

If you really want to make the most of the favors won from your partner, save them up and and make him or her carry them out over the next few days. This takes the game into a different league. In order to avoid cheating, or 'forgetting,'

▼ *Erotic card games give you the opportunity to indulge in your wildest fantasies, such as gentle bondage, unusual positions or oral sex.*

▲ *Everyone's a winner in strip poker because both of you end up naked, aroused and ready to make love at the climax of the game.*

you will need to create 'favor' chips to gamble with. The easiest way to do this is to fold the favor, written on paper, and secure it with tape. Write down anything you like – from 'wash the dishes for a day' to 'massage my back with scented oil for one hour'.

SLAVE FOR A NIGHT
Alternatively, you could play for just one big favor – the loser becomes the winner's slave for a night. The winner can decide when and where to make love, which position, or combination of positions to choose, and how long you make love for.

If poker doesn't appeal, there are plenty of other games you can play instead. Choose something that you both enjoy, but make it simple and fun. Remember, the object is to double your pleasure by combining the thrill of the game with the prize of your partner, so deal the cards, roll the dice and have a wild night! ❤

RUDE FOOD

If food is your fantasy, why not take a selection of what you enjoy and partake in an erotic feast, with your partner as the main course.

▲ For those who like it sweet and sticky – try drizzling syrup or honey over your partner's erogenous zones and then lick it off with tantalizing sweeps of the tongue that will turn oral sex into a sugary delight.

Taste is an essential sense in the sexual act. Along with touch, sight, hearing and smell, it completes our sensual map of our partner and makes the experience of lovemaking complete. Additional stimulation of any of the senses can add an extra dimension to your sex life, and taste, in particular, can be enhanced by including your favorite foods in your sexual games.

Whipped cream, ice-cream, chocolate spread and cream cheese – a little of what you fancy, spread enticingly across your partner's body, or used to tease and tempt during lovemaking, can be deeply erotic. But above all food can be fun, when the object of the game is to taste, lick and kiss your partner clean. The only preparation necessary is to cover the bed or rug with a large beach towel, and to have plenty of tissues ready to mop up any spills.

Whipped cream is one of the most sensual of all sweet toppings. Its rich, creamy flavor makes it a delicious addition to any dessert, but better still its cool, mousse-like texture feels gloriously smooth and silky on warm skin.

To indulge yourself in some whipped cream fun, treat your partner like a giant sundae. Lay them down in a comfortable position and prepare to spray the cream across the length of their body. For him, start at the chest with whorls and patterns, then apply a thick, soft, piled line down to the navel. For her, cover the breasts in peaks and mounds – you could even finish with a cherry on each nipple or in the navel.

Work fast, as the cream has a tendency to melt as soon as it comes into contact with body heat. The extravagant can decorate still further, with silver balls, cake sprinkles, fruit such as peaches, strawberries and cherries, or chocolate flakes to create the ultimate in dream desserts.

DOS AND DON'TS

DO SPREAD A PROTECTIVE COVER OVER THE BED OR THE FLOOR BEFORE YOU BEGIN TO PROTECT AGAINST MESSY SPILLS.

DON'T SPREAD FOOD OVER SENSITIVE AREAS IF YOUR PARTNER DOESN'T LIKE IT. IF ANYTHING STARTS TO HURT OR STING, WASH IT OFF IMMEDIATELY WITH A MILD SOAP AND WARM WATER.

DO WASH BEFORE YOU MAKE LOVE WITH A CONDOM, AS MANY FOOD SUBSTANCES CAN PERISH THE RUBBER AND REDUCE THE CONDOM'S EFFECTIVENESS IN MINUTES.

DON'T OVERDO IT. SOME FOODS ARE SO RICH THAT IF YOU EAT TOO MUCH OF THEM YOU MAY FIND YOURSELF TOO QUEASY TO MAKE LOVE.

Once the topping is complete, you can begin the delightful task of eating your creation. Begin with a silver spoon, gently running the cool of the metal down the center of their body, circling the navel, then down between the thighs, offering your partner small mouthfuls as you go.

When the temperature really heats up, you can meet fire with ice and share a tub of exotic ice-cream or frozen yogurt. Allow a spoonful to soften slightly, then let it slide slowly down her

cleavage – it should provoke shivers of delight. Try the effect on different parts of the body to test the response – the back, the inner arms, the thighs and even the feet. For him, take a spoonful in your mouth and then, once you have eaten it, slowly run your tongue along his penis. The cold of your mouth should elicit a cry of joyful pain! Do the same for her – take a spoonful or two of ice-cream or yogurt, swallow it, and while your tongue is still freezing, treat her to oral sex.

Honey, maple syrup and karo syrup are the ultimate sweeteners, and can add extra flavor to your lovemaking.

▶ *Let a spoonful of ice-cream soften against your partner's warm skin, then scoop it up to shivers of delight.*

▼ *Take your time with the feast and lick every inch of ice-cream away, your tongue caressing each nook and cranny.*

whatever you prefer, together with tiny glasses which you can use more as a pouring utensil than a drinking vessel. Pour the crystal or creamy liquid, drop by drop, into your partner's navel, across their nipples, and between their toes.

SAVORY SEX

Sweetness is not to everyone's taste, so for those who prefer their sex a little more savory, try olive oil, peanut butter or salad dressings – you can raid the refrigerator for imaginative ideas. Daub each flavor in a new place, then explore them with your tongue, kissing and licking the remains of the food from your partner's body.

A SEA OF PLEASURE

Seafood is often thought to have aphrodisiac properties, and for many their delicate salty flavor is infinitely preferable to the sweetness of chocolate and cream. With seafood such as mussels, oysters and prawns you have a chance to create a sensual extravaganza. Buy a selection from your local shop or supermarket, complete with accompanying dips and sauces. Then when you are ready to feast, make your partner comfortable, and slowly lay a seafood banquet across their body. Arrange each morsel in a precise fashion or exotic pattern across the chest or breasts, the arms, the stomach and the thighs. Add the sauce and the garnish to each little section – you can take your time as seafood does not melt or drip.

Once your work of art is finished, you are both free to enjoy the fruits of your labor. The chef is free to feed his or her masterwork piece by piece to the captive, or to eat each item one by one from the captive's body. This can be done by hand or with the mouth alone. Work until all the seafood has been devoured – and then you can start to devour your partner. ❤

▼ Use whipped cream, ice-cream or frozen yogurt to please your partner at the climax to your erotic feast. Take it in turns to play 'dessert' and then you can make sweet, sticky love for the rest of the night.

Like the whipped cream, the application is as much fun as the removal. With a spoon, drizzle the syrup of your choice over your partner's skin. Weave fine strands over his penis or her genitals to make oral sex a sugary delight. Chocaholics can do the same with chocolate sauce.

Liqueurs are the ultimate sweet, sticky after-dinner drink; rich and potent, and deliciously wicked. Take

SNAP HAPPY

Load up your camera, dress up your partner and get ready to play photographer and model. Not only will you have a good time, but you may get some good pictures into the bargain!

aking sexy photographs of your partner is something that everyone who owns a camera can try. It can be tremendous fun and a great turn-on. With today's equipment you don't have to be an expert to get good results, and your pictures will be a lasting testimony to those moments of love and laughter.

FIRST THINGS FIRST
Before you consider where and how you are going to take your photographs, you need to consider how or where you are

▲ *Experiment with different camera and lighting angles to highlight the parts of your partner's body that you like best.*

◀ *Don't be afraid to dress up – or down! – for the camera. Sexy underwear, and props such as whips, will enhance the final photo.*

going to get them developed, as this will dictate the kind of pictures you can take. If you have access to a darkroom and can develop your own prints, or have an instant Polaroid camera, there is

no limit to the poses, positions or state of undress of your subject.

But if you intend to take your films to a standard laboratory for processing, you will have to be a little more restrained.

◀ *Vary the style and mood of your shots. Ask your partner to 'direct' you through different poses and positions. Whether it is a romantic or raunchy feel you want, playing suitable music will put you in the right frame of mind.*

Explicit pictures featuring genitalia and sexual intercourse are generally considered to be 'obscene' and can be destroyed by the lab. However, most would not object to developing more straightforward sexy pictures or artistic photographs. As a general rule, if it is permitted on television, it is permitted in your prints.

WHICH CAMERA?

Each kind of camera will give you a different result. What you can achieve with a Polaroid will differ dramatically from what you can achieve with a compact camera, or a single lens reflex.

▶ *Going through a striptease routine as your partner clicks away will provide sexy frame-by-frame shots.*

With a Polaroid camera, the results are instant. You have no control over the lighting – a flash will fire if the camera senses there is not enough light. But the slightly fuzzy quality of the final print can work to your advantage. Curves and lines are softened and flattered, and the flash tends to even out the tones of the skin. And of course, the greatest advantage of a Polaroid is that the only limit to the kind of shots you can take is your imagination!

▼ *Hopefully you'll feel sufficiently relaxed with your partner to act out your fantasies and really let yourself go.*

Compact cameras with built-in flashes are the easiest cameras to use as they regulate everything for you, but this often means you have no control over the results. The flash that is designed

AS LARGE AS LIFE

STAND YOUR PARTNER AGAINST A PLAIN BACKGROUND (A SHEET HUNG OVER A DOOR AND DRAPED PART-WAY OVER THE FLOOR WILL DO) OR LAY THEM ON A PLAIN BEDCOVER. THEN, WORKING FROM THE SAME ANGLE ALL THE WAY DOWN, SHOOT EVERY PART OF THE BODY. THIS WILL BE FUN IN ITSELF, BUT NOT NEARLY AS MUCH FUN AS PUTTING THE PICTURE TOGETHER LIKE AN EROTIC JIGSAW WHEN THE PHOTOGRAPHS ARE DEVELOPED.

Then, once you have warmed them up with a few simple poses, you can start to direct a little more carefully. If they are dressed, for example, ask them to remove an article of clothing very slowly, and take a series of photographs to give you a frame-by-frame striptease show you can enjoy at any time.

STRIKE A POSE

Photographs are also a golden opportunity to indulge in another kind of fun – that of dressing up. Think about your sexual heroes or heroines. You can adopt the clothes and the look, and with a bit of make-up or styling become Madonna, Marilyn Monroe, one of the Chippendales or a Viking. Get in position in front of the lens, strike a pose, then marvel (or laugh) at the results! ♥

to light party scenes and night-time objects can prove too bright for the naked body, which needs a much more careful and softer approach. Why not try the trick the professionals use and stretch a black stocking over the lens? This gives a wonderful soft-focus effect to the prints, adding atmosphere and mood to the shots.

Single lens reflex 35mm cameras are the most flexible and can be used for wonderful artistic shots, but again, the lighting is of prime importance. Use natural daylight if you can, experimenting with shadows to create fabulous areas of light and dark across the body.

SPONTANEOUS SNAPS

Often, simplicity is the best policy, and spontaneous snaps work as well as carefully-prepared shots. Pick a moment when your partner is particularly happy and relaxed, then just snap away. Encourage them to pose in clothes they feel comfortable in – a silk dressing gown that slips casually off her shoulder or a small towel wound around his waist.

▲ *Cameras fitted with a time-delay allow both you and your partner to have fun acting out some photo-fantasies.*

▶ *For a natural look, try not to be too conscious of the camera and indulge in some spontaneous lovemaking.*

MAKING A SEXY VIDEO

Making an erotic video can be a wonderful experience, allowing you both a new and exciting perspective on your love life.

▼ *The scene is set...*
Lights! Camera! Action!

Making your own erotic video should be fun as well as titillating. Not only does it give you the chance to see yourselves making love, it also enables you both to direct and star in your own movie.

GETTING READY

Much of the pleasure in making a video will be in the preparation. The more effort you put into the film, the better your end result will be.

First, you both need to familiarize yourselves with the workings of the camera. Try firing off a few feet of video on test shots. It will not be wasted as you can always record over it again. You also need to practice to make sure that you get the focus and framing right.

Of course your video is not going to be restricted to showing each partner in turn. You will need some scenes where the two of you are on screen together. These are best filmed using a tripod, so that you have a full range of adjustments for the position of the camera.

Next, rehearse certain scenes and take up various positions with your partner without leaving the frame. This

will require a little practice, but you will quickly find that you develop a sense for playing to the camera.

Although the image of two people making love is in itself interesting, your video will have a more long-lasting appeal if it has a strong story-line.

It is best to write a rough shooting script so that each of you knows what to do. This could include lines of dialogue, camera and stage directions. But don't

THE STORY BOARD

PROFESSIONAL FILM MAKERS TURN THEIR SCRIPTS INTO A STORY BOARD – A CARTOON STRIP SHOWING EACH SCENE AND CAMERA SHOT. THIS DETAILED APPROACH MAY NOT BE NECESSARY FOR A HOME VIDEO, BUT IF YOU CAME ACROSS SOME IMAGES OR POSES YOU PARTICULARLY LIKED IN YOUR TEST SHOTS, A STORY BOARD WILL HELP YOU COMBINE THEM WITH THE MAIN STORY LINE OF YOUR VIDEO.

◀ For scenes which include both of you, look through the lens first to check the exact area which is in frame. Then you can start filming and move into shot yourself.

straightforward striptease – simply because one partner can handle the camera while the other supplies the action. But try and be inventive. Move the camera and alter the framing. Try striptease on the move, down a corridor or up and down the stairs.

If you can, move the camera around your partner and film them from all angles as they remove their clothes. The stripper can either be unconscious of the camera, as if they were simply undressing in the privacy of their own home, or they can be very seductive and

make these too hard and fast – you should leave room for improvisation.

Next you need to decide on the location. Probably you will want to use your own house as you are going to need privacy, so plan out which corners are going to suit the action.

Remember that if you are filming in a room, at most you can only show two of the walls at any one time. Pick the best two. But also be inventive. You may be able to take some interesting shots up and down the staircase and through windows and doors.

ALTERED IMAGES

The camera need not always be at chest height either. Interesting shots can be achieved shooting upwards from the floor, or down from the ceiling – or reflected in a strategically placed mirror.

Remember too, that in the absence of any powerful and expensive artificial lighting you are going to have to rely on sunlight, so use the room with the biggest windows.

Keep your shooting script handy throughout filming and try to stick to it. But if something exciting occurs, capture the moment on tape. It may be better than anything you had planned.

The easiest scenario to film is a

DOS AND DON'TS

• *DON'T* ZOOM IN AND THEN OUT AGAIN. THE EFFECT OF THESE 'YO-YO' SHOTS IS VERY UNSETTLING.

• *DO* VARY YOUR ZOOM LENGTHS AND SPEEDS. SLOW ZOOMS CONCENTRATE INTEREST; FAST ONES GIVE SHOCK EFFECTS.

• *DO* MARK OUT THE AREA 'IN FRAME' FOR SHOTS WHEN BOTH OF YOU ARE ON SCREEN UNTIL YOU ARE USED TO THE CAMERA.

• *DO* DEVISE YOUR OWN EXOTIC OR SEXY COSTUMES AND MAKE-UP TO GO WITH YOUR DIFFERENT STORYLINES.

▶ Use the zoom lens to take smooth, erotic close-ups of part of your partner's body. The zoom concentrates interest and has a powerful effect, so be careful not to overuse it.

imagination. If the camera follows the feet of a subject upstairs while clothes fall around them on the steps, the viewer will draw only one conclusion.

CAMERA AND ACTION

If you do not have any editing facilities, you are going to be restricted when filming actual intercourse. Most video cameras do not have remote control facilities, so you may need to devise your scene so that one of you has a reason to walk on to the set at the beginning – after switching the camera on – and then off again at the end to turn it off.

The pleasure of a video is not just in the making of it – watching the results of your efforts should be just as much fun. You and your partner should watch the raw tape – the rushes – deciding which shots should be kept and which cut out.

Once you have the final version ready, you should make quite an occasion of the first showing. Have a glass of wine, close the curtains, dim the lights, and watch your movie on a comfortable sofa or in bed. You may find that you want to relive some of the highlights of your own personal love tape! ♥

▲ Pulling back from her passion-filled face to a wide-angled shot which shows the reason for her passion can be very effective.

▼ ▶ Once you are accustomed to the lens, you will gain confidence in being your own film star. Just lie back and let the cameras roll!

play up to the camera as if they were doing a sexy striptease to turn on a lover.

A portable camera can also 'discover' a subject. It can come in through the bathroom door and find a naked man taking a bath, or look through a window to see a naked girl combing her hair.

LONG, SLOW AND SEXY

Panning slowly across a naked body, from head to toe – or from toe to head – can have a lingering eroticism, as can panning slowly across the scene to find a nude in a far corner.

What is not seen is often more erotic than what is – such is the power of

EXPLORE YOURSELF

The first step on the way to sexual fulfillment is getting to know yourself – intimately. Lock yourself away, dim the lights, light the scented candles and let your fingers do the walking...

Exploring your own body is an exciting way of discovering what turns you on. You can use this knowledge to improve your sexual relationship and to increase your pleasure during masturbation.

Getting to know your own body is a wonderful first step to a more satisfying sexual relationship. Many women have no idea what their genitals look like and even those who masturbate regularly may always use the same method and be unaware that other types of stimulation can be equally enjoyable. Setting aside a regular time to explore, experiment and pleasure yourself can re-awaken sexual feelings and make you feel more sexually confident. Once you know what type of touch most turns you on, you'll be able to communicate this to your partner and improve your lovemaking.

In order to explore your body you need a warm, comfortable room and guaranteed peace and quiet, so there's no point in doing it when the kids are due home from school. You'll need to be naked, so after a bath would be ideal. You could dim the lights, play soft music and burn scented candles to get yourself in the mood. Or why not buy some sensuous aromatherapy

▶ **Lock the door, take the phone off the hook, have a long, hot, relaxing bath and get to know your body.**

oils and heat them in a burner? Ylang ylang is particularly recommended as an aphrodisiac.

FROM HEAD TO TOE

Once you are comfortable and relaxed, explore all over your body, not just those parts usually associated with sexual pleasure. Take time to really feel the textures of skin and hair on different parts of your body. Notice if any areas feel particularly pleasing to touch – you may discover erogenous zones you never even realized you had before.

Then move onto your breasts, running your hands over them. What feels better – a firm or gentle touch?

Use your fingers to circle your nipples – what sort of touch makes them erect? As you experiment with different movements, it may help if you lick your fingers for lubrication, or dip them in some scented massage oil or moisturizing cream.

EXPLORING YOUR GENITALS

After the breasts move onto your genital area. Start by feeling your inner thighs; notice how soft the skin is and remember to register how each touch makes you feel. Run your hands over your hips and bottom. When you are ready you can start to explore your genitals. If you want to see what you are doing, sit up against some cushions

▲ *If you don't get to know yourself, how can anyone else?*

▼ *Explore your skin slowly, inch by inch, and make all the stops along the way.*

▼ You may begin to discover more ways of turning yourself on than you ever knew existed.

and use a small hand-held mirror. First you will be able to see the hair-covered outer lips or labia majora. If you part these you will see the pink fleshy inner lips or labia minora. These meet at the top of the vulva to form the clitoral hood which covers the exquisitely sensitive clitoris, below which lies the entrance to the vagina.

Once you have familiarized yourself with what it all looks like, concentrate on where and how you most like to be touched. It's important that your fingers are well lubricated. If you are already aroused you will be wet enough; otherwise use a little baby oil. Take your time exploring the labia. Which feels best, firm or gentle

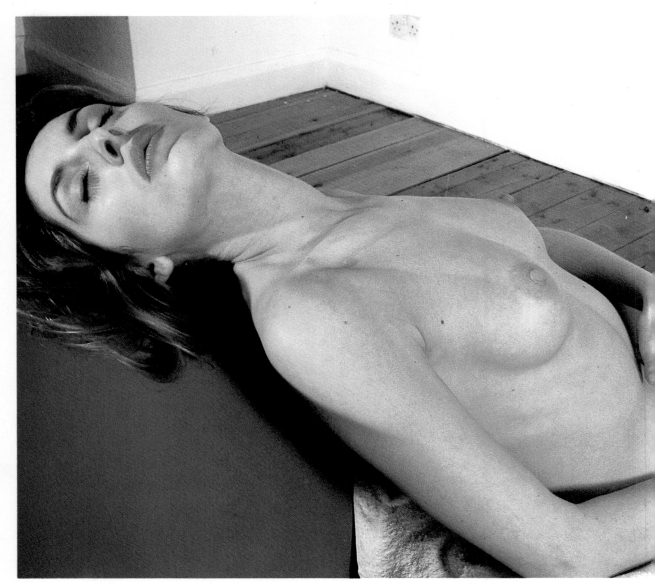

stroking? Experiment with speed of touch and try using the side of your hand as well as your fingers.

EXPLORING ORGASM

It's well worth spending time on your clitoris. Many men know where it is but have only a vague idea what they are supposed to do with it. Although the clitoris is small you will find that touching the base and tip produces very different feelings. Sometimes the tip is so sensitive that direct stimulation becomes painful. Try rubbing and stroking, hard and fast or soft and gentle. Sometimes the best sensations are produced if the clitoris is stimulated indirectly through the clitoral hood or by squeezing your legs together to exert pressure on it.

Next try inserting a finger into your vagina, making sure you are well lubricated. You may enjoy the sensation of thrusting your fingers in and out or prefer a more gentle touch. If your finger is long enough you may be able to stimulate your own G spot. It's located on the front wall of the vagina about two thirds of the way up and can sometimes be felt as a spongy cushion of muscle. The G spot responds best to a fairly firm touch. Start off gently and increase the pressure until you feel something.

By this stage of your exploration you will probably feel really turned on and be wanting to have an orgasm – go ahead! Next time experiment with different ways of bringing yourself to orgasm. Do some ways of touching feel more pleasurable than others? ❤

▲ *Exploring your own body is great preparation for sex with your partner.*

WHY NOT...

• EXPERIMENT WITH DIFFERENT TEXTURED MATERIAL AGAINST YOUR BREASTS AND THIGHS. SILK, FUR, SATIN OR VELVET CAN BE DELICIOUSLY SENSUAL.

• INVEST IN A VIBRATOR AND TRY IT OUT ALL OVER YOUR BODY. VARY THE SPEED AND SEE HOW IT FEELS OVER YOUR BREASTS, BOTTOM AND THIGHS.

• IMAGINE SOMEONE IS WATCHING YOU, OBSERVING AND LEARNING WHAT TURNS YOU ON. THIS IS AN EXCITING FANTASY AND ONE WHICH MANY MEN WOULD ENJOY TURNING INTO REALITY.

FINDING THE G SPOT

The G spot has caused much heated discussion. Does it exist? Where is it? What is it? Most important of all, does it really produce mind-blowing vaginal orgasms?

▲ *Kneeling and then leaning back on to her heels is a good position for a woman to adopt when finding her G spot.*

Although the clitoris is acknowledged as the principal source of sexual satisfaction in women, some researchers claim that there is also a small bean-shaped patch of erectile tissue situated a short way up the front wall of the vagina which can produce orgasms when stimulated. This area – called the G spot after Ernst Grafenberg, the German gynecologist who discovered it in the 1940s – is said to be directly behind the pubic bone and ½–1in across. It is controversial because while some sexual experts say it does exist, some say not every woman has one – they think it may just be a physical peculiarity that some women have and others don't. Others believe its existence is a myth.

Controversy aside, 25 per cent of women do report having vaginal orgasms and many of them believe they are triggered by the G spot.

50

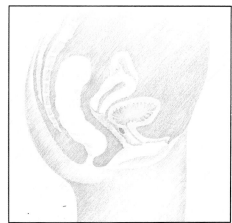

Finding your G spot can lead to seriously sexy loveplay – if you find it, good; if you don't, you'll have fun!

FINDING YOUR G SPOT

Start your exploration on your own: nobody knows your body better than you. Lie face down on the bed with a pillow under your hips, lubricate your fingers – or a vibrator – and insert them into your vagina. If you hold one hand on the lower part of your stomach and apply slight pressure, you'll be able to feel what's happening more. Curl your index finger about three inches up inside you and press back against the wall of the vagina in a 'come here' motion. If you locate the spot the feeling may be slightly uncomfortable at first, because you won't be familiar with the sensation. Don't expect that you will orgasm immediately!

You can try this self-exploration lying on your back or you could try doing it in a squatting position. You may feel the urge to pee, so you could try locating the G spot in the bathroom!

LET YOUR PARTNER EXPLORE

You can discover your G spot alone but it will be much more fun with your partner. It will be incredibly

▲ *If the woman raises her hips with a pillow, her partner can find her G spot with his fingers.*

▲ *Top right: This diagram shows where the G spot (marked in red) is usually found in women.*

▼ *The woman may prefer her partner to use his fingers rather than his penis to stimulate her.*

stimulating for both of you if he watches you touch yourself and then does it himself. Don't be at all embarrassed to ask him – he'll enjoy it. Trying to find your G spot will enhance sex for both of you; you'll get more pleasure and he'll love giving you more pleasure.

Show him where you feel the best sensation and then let him touch you. Lie down, facing down or up, place a pillow beneath your hips, open your legs and let him place his fingers inside you, feeling for your most sensitive spot. Watching you writhe and knowing he's learning more about your body and pleasure will be very arousing for both of you.

Once you feel you've located the spot, try touching it with his penis while in different positions. Here are some suggestions:

STIMULATING POSITIONS

• Most rear-entry positions hit the right spot because the penis is able to press against the front wall of your vagina. Let him lie on top of you and re-locate your G spot himself, with his penis.

• Another, even more erotic position is if you half-squat on the edge of the bed and let him enter you from behind.

• Lie facing each other. Hook your top leg over his hip and pull him toward you with your thigh, letting his penis slide into you – he'll be able to stimulate your G spot and caress and kiss you at the same time.

In addition to helping you have great sex, a lot of fun, and hopefully a

▲ *Rear-entry positions enable the man to pinpoint his partner's G spot.*

▼ *This position allows for exactly the right angle of penetration.*

lifetime of earth-shattering orgasms, stimulation of the G spot is also alleged to produce an ejaculatory fluid during orgasm; some women even urinate. Don't worry or get embarrassed if you do urinate or release a lot of fluid; just enjoy it as part of the wonderful sexiness of orgasm. Happy searching. ♥

BLINDFOLD GAMES

We all touch, hear, taste and feel more intensely in the dark. By putting on a blindfold and depriving our sense of sight, we can experience and explore a whole new range of exquisite sensations and feelings.

DOS AND DON'TS

DO TRY MUTUAL MASTURBATION WITH YOU AND YOUR PARTNER BOTH WEARING BLINDFOLDS. YOU COULD TRY LOCKING YOUR LEGS TOGETHER, LYING ON THE BED SO THAT YOU CAN FEEL EACH OTHER'S MOVEMENTS.

DO PLAY BLINDFOLD GAMES WHEN YOU ARE OUTSIDE AT THE BEACH. TRY SIFTING HANDFULS OF FINE SAND OVER THE BACKS OF YOUR LOVER'S LEGS OR UP AND DOWN THEIR ARMS.

DON'T KEEP THE GAME GOING IF YOUR PARTNER WANTS YOU TO STOP BECAUSE HE OR SHE IS FEELING UNCOMFORTABLE.

DON'T PLACE TOXIC OR NON-FOOD SUBSTANCES IN YOUR LOVER'S MOUTH TO TRY AND MAKE HIM OR HER IDENTIFY THEM.

▲ *Our sense of sight defines the world around us. Take it away temporarily and our other senses have to work harder to compensate. This can be used to great effect when it comes to the tactile realm of love play. So get your blindfolds ready...*

The way we react to people and situations which we can see with our eyes has a profound effect on how we behave. Yet, if sight is taken away, even for a short period of time, we can 'see' with our other four senses more fully and intensely. Try it out for yourself with some simple blindfold games.

The blindfolds themselves can be made of any material, but the smoothest and most sensual material is probably silk – a silk scarf is perfect. Decide who will be the first to take a turn, then the 'sighted' partner can tie the scarf around the 'blind' partner's head.

TOUCH AND FEEL

First, explore your sense of touch. Try different textures to tantalize your partner. Feathers, and bits of velvet, silk and linen are good to start with. Have your partner lie on his or her back and then slowly begin to tickle the back of their neck. Work your way down the

▲ With your eyes blindfolded, your taste buds will be at their most acute. Why not have 'blind' tastings, using each other's body as the table!

can apply a bit more pressure on this area as it is quite tough.

Now gently massage the front of their neck and slowly work your way down to the breasts or chest. Massage the area carefully in small circles starting with the nipples and then moving in larger circles.

Swish your hands down to the waist and hips and massage the tummy. Finally, move down and gently stroke the genital area, making sure your fin-

length of their spine with feather-light strokes, then heavier brush strokes. Tickle the back of their calves with a bit of velvet, alternating with the other materials. Try brushing his or her buttocks with a soft baby brush.

Now turn them over to stimulate their sensitive front. For women: lightly dust her nipples and the area around her breasts with a piece of linen. Its slightly rough texture will make her tingle. For men: wind a piece of silk loosely around his penis and then slowly unwind it.

Brush the inside of their legs with wide, gentle strokes. Come seductively close to their genitals and then change tactics when they least expect it.

EXTRA-SENSUAL MASSAGE

There is nothing more sensual than a long, deep and lingering massage. If you are the masseur or masseuse, coat your hands with deliciously scented oil, perhaps vanilla, orange or musk. While your partner stands naked and blindfolded in front of you, spread your hands across their shoulders and slowly smear the oil down their back. Rub their buttocks in an up and down motion – you

WHY NOT...

PLAY BLIND MAN'S BLUFF BY TRYING TO 'PIN' BITS OF STICKY LICORICE TO YOUR LOVER'S NAKED BODY. SCORE POINTS FOR THE MOST AROUSING TARGETS 'PINNED,' THEN EAT THEM OFF EACH OTHER.

LET YOUR PARTNER STAND NAKED BEFORE YOU AND SPRAY THEM WITH A WATER PISTOL OR PLANT SPRAY GUN. ALTERNATE THE WATER PRESSURE AS YOU SPRAY THEM ALL OVER THEIR BODY.

SET UP A BLINDFOLD WINE TASTING TREAT – OR TRY A CHOCOLATE TASTING SESSION WITH YOUR LOVER'S FAVORITE RICH AND SUMPTUOUS TRUFFLES.

PREPARE A BLINDFOLD FEAST FOR YOU AND YOUR LOVER. MAKE A RULE THAT YOU MUST REMAIN BLINDFOLDED THROUGHOUT THE ENTIRE DINNER.

gers are well oiled. Anything can happen from this point on.

OH SO DELICIOUS

You can play a taste game where your lover must taste various foods and then guess what they are. Use fresh fruits, oysters, chocolates and salty foods such as nuts or pretzels. Try dabbing honey, maple syrup or ice-cream on the tip of their tongue. Or prepare a couple of their favorite dishes and then let them guess the ingredients.

Have your partner wait in a darkened room blindfolded as you raid the kitchen. Place little morsels of food in their mouth, or perhaps just smear them across their lips for a brief moment. If they like the food, you can feed them more of it in tiny bits. Tease them with kisses in between these bites.

BLINDFOLD FINALE

Try making love to your partner while he or she is blindfolded. The new sensations which this can bring can be quite amazing. We usually depend very much on our sight for erotic stimulation but by

removing this sense we can heighten and accentuate the others deliciously.

Give your other senses an extra treat by having some soft music playing in the background as you settle back on to some plump cushions or a bed. Keep feathers, scarves and scented oils handy so that you can carry on the love play, if you wish, or put on a blindfold yourself and join in the fun. ❤

▲ *If water pistols are just for children, then bring out the child in yourself and 'shoot' your blindfolded partner.*

◄ *Caressing, undressing, massaging and then making love to your blindfolded partner will produce amazing sensations. Take it in turns to be the 'sighted' partner.*

FEATHER FANTASIA

Ostrich plumes, peacock feathers and those wonderful filmstar boas... Few can resist the allure of feathers, so why not pluck yourself a handful and tickle your partner's fancy with an exotic evening of teasing and titillation?

The bright, jewel colors and exotic fronds of bird feathers have featured in the grandest costumes and accessories throughout the world. Brash and vibrant, or subtle and downy, they look and feel fabulous against smooth warm skin, and the light caress of a fluffy frond can add a new dimension to your lovemaking.

FANTASTIC FEELINGS

Feathers can be a principal ingredient in the most sensuous of games. Their delicate fronds can be used to elicit the most delicious sensations when floated across your partner's body. And it is not only the erogenous zones which succumb – every inch of the skin can be made to quiver under the power of the plume.

Most fabric stores and florists carry a good selection of dyed and treated feathers. Choose one in a color and shape that appeals to you, then prepare to put it into action. First make your partner warm, relaxed and comfortable with a bit of pampering. Gently remove their clothes and lay them naked on the bed or a soft rug on the floor. A blindfold can help intensify the sensation of touch by cutting out vision, and for a real treat, place

stereo headphones over their ears, plug them in and switch them on to their favorite music.

Make sure you are comfortable too before you start so that you can give the longest feather stroke possible. Kneel or sit beside your partner's head, and begin.

EXQUISITE TORTURE

Start at the top, running the feather slowly and lightly across the forehead, down to the tip of the nose, then over the top lip – linger on this particular spot for a while as it is extremely sensitive to the feather's delicate fronds.

Then tickle the ears, one at a time, until your partner can stand it no longer. From the ears, move down across the jawline to the chin, then spiraling the feather down the neck and on to the body. Lightly dust the chest or breasts, caress the nipples with the very tip, then whip it away quickly just to tease.

◀ ▲ ▶ A simple blindfold can open the way to a garden of new delights. It's also a great way for both of you to overcome any inhibitions which might make you too shy to let go and enjoy yourself.

Stroke the rest of the body, swirling your feathers over the thighs, the arms, the wrists, the knees. Use just the tip for a delicate, teasing stroke and the full plume for a rich, soft caress.

DIFFERENT STROKES

To induce a state of shivering excitement, lift the feather away and touch it again to another area, so that your partner never knows what to expect. If you want to soothe your partner into deep, melting sensuality, use a long, slow stroke that never loses contact with the skin.

◀ ▲ Running the fronds of a soft plume over the contours of your partner's body is a wonderful way to explore their reactions and appreciate their beauty.

Once you have completed one side of the body, turn your partner over and start on the next. When you have given them as much tickling as they can take, go for the grand finale – the feet!

FROM TOP TO TOE

Run the feather over the sole, along the tips of the toes, across the top of the foot and round the ankle. Push the tip of the quill into those sensitive areas between the toes and pull the rest of the feather through after it. Use the quill again to press gently on the sole, running the point up and down the arch of the foot and around the base of the toes. Find out where your partner is most susceptible to the pleasure – or the agony – of the teasing fronds and play on it for as long as both of you can stand it.

FEATHER BOAS

For many show artistes, a feather boa is an integral part of their act. The slow, rippling movement of those hundreds of fronds enhances the movement in the dance, and the long, fluffy mass offers plenty to hide behind when the artiste would otherwise be baring all.

Lush, brilliantly colored boas are available in all fabric stores, and a single length, or even several boas woven together can create a spectacular sex accessory. Women can use a boa effectively as a wonderful prelude to lovemaking. Just wrap the mass of feathers seductively around your naked body and proceed to dance, never quite revealing what your partner longs to see. When he can stand it no more, let him unwrap you like a precious gift. ❤

FEATHER GAMES

ONCE YOU HAVE DISPENSED WITH THE BOA, THE SMALL, LOOSE FEATHERS SHED IN ALL THE FUN CAN ALSO BE USED AS A GAME. SIT WITH A SMALL PILE BETWEEN YOU BOTH, THEN ON A COUNT OF THREE, SCATTER THEM IN THE AIR. THE OBJECT IS THEN TO BLOW THE FEATHERS AS HARD AS YOU CAN AWAY FROM YOU AND ON TO YOUR PARTNER. WHEN ALL THE FEATHERS HAVE COME TO REST, COUNT UP HOW MANY HAVE LANDED ON EACH OF YOU. THE ONE WITH THE LEAST FEATHERS GETS TO CHOOSE A FORFEIT – WHICH THE LOSER HAS TO PERFORM. OF COURSE, IF YOU'RE FEELING PARTICULARLY CRUEL, YOU COULD MAKE THEM PERFORM A FORFEIT FOR EVERY FEATHER...

SOFT BONDAGE

One of the great sexual fantasies of all time, bondage can be wildly erotic and deeply passionate, adding that hint of danger, spice and abandon to your lovemaking.

▲ *Start by wrapping a band of soft silk around the wrists and ankles so that there is no danger of chafing. Let your fingertips skate over your partner's erogenous zones, then repeat the exercise with your lips.*

Bondage is a commonly occurring theme in many sexual fantasies. But while some couples are happy to leave it within the realms of their imagination, others use it occasionally, or even regularly, to add a little spice to their sex lives. The ultimate sex game, bondage embodies the elements of power, domination, submission and surrender. Undertaken gently, and in the spirit of fun, there is no reason why it should be harmful to your relationship, provided of course that both part-

ners are happy with the game and their roles within it.

The idea is not to hurt, or even create discomfort, but simply to immobilize your partner, making them completely helpless and at your mercy.

An old-fashioned bed – a four-poster or a Victorian-style brass bed – is the ideal setting for a night of bound passion. However, anything which has pillars or bars at each corner will suffice. If your bed is of the simple kind without a headboard, don't despair – with a little

▶ *With her hands gently bound, and her body facing away from you, caress her as you enter her from behind. But talk and tease first, as this can be one of the most tantalizing things about soft bondage.*

▼ *Once you have bound your partner safely, feel free to experiment, but progress slowly so that you are sure that neither one is putting undue pressure on the other to partake in anything they are not sure about.*

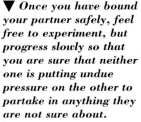

ingenuity long cords can even be draped over the edge of the bed and attached to the wheels under the box spring!

Choose soft materials as bindings – silken dressing-gown cords, featherlight chiffon scarves, stockings or strips of lace. You can theme it – the adventurous can use climbing ropes, naughty school-girls or boys can use ties, cowboys or Indians leather thongs, and doctors and nurses clean white bandages.

You may find that one of you prefers to do the tying, while the other prefers to be tied. Or perhaps you prefer to take it in turns to bind each other. Whichever way suits you, make sure you do it care-fully so as not to hurt the skin.

WHEN HE IS TIED . . .

His whole body is yours to explore and discover as he lies there bound and helpless. You can tempt and tease to

Whichever kind of bondage you choose, the most important thing to remember is that it should be a pleasure for you both. Should either of you wish to stop, you should stop immediately. But for many couples, a dabble into the realms of fantasy adds an extra dimension to their sexual partnership. ❤

▲ *Slowly remove your clothes in front of your partner, then caress and tease him – while he cannot move, you hold all the power.*

your heart's desire. There is no need even to touch him. You have the power to inflame him simply by being there. Undress in front of him, or dress up in something he really likes. Then run your fingers up and down the length of his body. The fact that he cannot reciprocate will drive him wild. When you know he can hold out no longer, give in to him, and guide him inside you.

WHEN SHE IS TIED . . .

She surrenders to you completely. Her body is open to you, and you have the power to please or deny. Cover her with kisses; let her feel the weight of your body on hers. Tease her with your tongue and give her the pleasure of long and sensual oral sex. Then enter her, and watch her pleasure as it mingles with the sweet frustration of being unable to touch your body.

DOS AND DON'TS

DO HAVE A KNIFE OR SHARP PAIR OF SCISSORS TO HAND, JUST IN CASE OF A REAL EMERGENCY.

DO HAVE A CODE WORD WHICH MEANS 'STOP, UNTIE ME IMMEDIATELY.' NORMAL PROTESTATIONS CAN OFTEN BE MISTAKEN FOR PART OF THE GAME.

DON'T TIE SCARVES OR CORDS TOO TIGHT. MAKE SURE THERE IS ENOUGH ROOM TO GET A FINGER BETWEEN WRISTS, ANKLES AND THE BINDINGS.

DON'T FALL ASLEEP AFTER SEX AND LEAVE YOUR PARTNER TIED UP. THIS IS VERY EASY TO DO, BUT CAN BE DANGEROUS.

▲ Penis-shaped drinking straws can add slurpy fun to your favourite drinks. Try preparing tasty food in the shape of a penis to carry on the theme.

▼ Sex toys come in all shapes and sizes – ranging from vibrators, phallic sponges and posing pouches to rude drinking straws and masks. Buy whatever takes your fancy and let the fun begin.

$\mathcal{S}$EX TOYS

When you are bored with board games on a Saturday night, sex toys can help you put frolicsome fun back into your naughty love play.

There is a vast choice of sex toys and aids for the couple who are looking for something a little bit different in their sex lives. They can add a new dimension to every aspect of your sensual foreplay. They can address every mood, from the highly erotic, to soft and romantic, to just good old-fashioned fun. Types of toys range from colorful, edible panties and condoms, to novelty props and clothes you can wear or place over the penis, breasts and female sex organs.

Special catalogues are available from which you can choose from any number of sex toys and paraphernalia, then purchase them by mail order. You can usu-

ally find advertisements for these companies in the backs of most women's and men's erotic magazines.

Alternatively, you may want to shop for sex toys together in a shop that sells erotic lingerie and sexy accessories. This option means you will be able to choose toys which appeal to both of you on sight, and will know what you are getting for your money.

Penis-shaped vibrators come in an amazing variety of sizes, textures and colors. From the quite small sized – about 4in long and ½in wide – to the deluxe jumbo-sized 7½in model, they are made to suit every woman. Some designs are hard and non-porous, while

others are soft, with a spongy flesh-like texture. A few have knobbly bits on the outside for added stimulation in the vagina, and some have clitoral stimulators attached to the base of the penis shape.

Many come with assorted attachments such as a G-spot massager and an anal stimulator. There is even a model moulded in the shape of a finger and thumb. Vibrators are designed to match her every mood and whim and can be used in conjunction with a partner or as a solo tool for masturbation.

Penis rings are another way to give a woman greater satisfaction. Usually

DOS AND DON'TS

DO MAKE YOUR OWN EDIBLE CONDOMS FROM FRUIT LEATHERS SOLD IN HEALTH FOOD SHOPS. SEW THE EDGES TOGETHER WITH SHOESTRING LICORICE.

DO BAKE YOUR LOVER A SEXY CAKE IN THE SHAPE OF THEIR FAVORITE BODY FEATURE. OR DECORATE A PLAIN CAKE WITH FROSTING PICTURES OF THE TWO OF YOU MAKING LOVE.

DON'T USE THE EDIBLE CONDOM AS A MEANS OF CONTRACEPTION. U.S. APPROVED CONDOMS MUST BE USED UNDER ALL NOVELTY ITEMS IF THEY ARE TO PREVENT PREGNANCY AND SEXUALLY TRANSMITTED DISEASES.

DON'T INSERT SHARP OR JAGGED ITEMS IN A WOMAN'S VAGINA. MOST SEX TOYS THAT YOU CAN PURCHASE ARE SAFE, BUT ALWAYS BE SURE THAT THERE ARE NO ROUGH EDGES WHICH MAY HAVE BEEN MISSED DURING SAFETY CHECKS.

▲ *Why not treat your man to a posing pouch – what better way to settle down to sex than by laughing together!*

▶ *Oral sex can be much more exciting and exhilarating when you literally tear off your lover's edible underwear with your mouth in a fit of animal hunger.*

made of plastic, they are placed over the man's erect penis before intercourse.

By wearing oriental love balls, a woman can feel pleasure at any time of the day. Ancient in origin but still popular today, these are little plastic or metal balls (with strings attached for safe removal), which are inserted into the vagina. As the woman moves, so do the the balls, stimulating the walls of the vagina and her G spot.

CARRY ON SEX

You can prepare a silly sex toy party in your own home for a light-hearted evening of intimate entertainment. Laughter is a wonderful and well-known aphrodisiac. Why not play tapes of your favorite comedy sketches and songs. Put yourselves into a silly mood with glasses which sport a penis nose. You can 'nose in' on your partner's most private parts.

At times you may desire your lover so much that you just want to eat them up. Edible items such as fruit-flavored panties and condoms can help you in your quest to 'devour' your loved one – they add a tasty twist to your sensuous games. With the aid of sex toys like the

▲ *Have some good clean fun by working each other up into a lather of love with penis-shaped sponges – they add a new and exhilarating dimension to bathing and showering together. Bath time will never be the same again!*

◀ *Both men and women adore the texture and taste of sensuous chocolate, so it's not surprising that it comes in many mischievous shapes – you can buy chocolate penises and testicles, as well as breast and vagina shapes.*

strap-on penis and pussy air-pump vagina, you can swap sexes with your partner and pretend you have become each other. Sex-swapping can lead to great role-play fun as you discover many of your lover's secret amorous desires by watching how they act as a member of the 'opposite sex.'

DO IT YOURSELF

Improvise your own sex toys with items you have lying around the house. Design your own rude t-shirts or nightshirts with fabric dye pens. You and your partner can wear them in bed, or under your work clothes for secret titillation. Long scarves make wonderful Tarzan and Jane-type loin cloths. Wrap the material around the waist and between the buttocks so that the cheeks stick out. With carefree abandon, you can carouse around the house, pretending that you are in the jungle. ♥

$\mathscr{S}$LIDE SHOW

If massage is your idea of heaven, take it to the limit with the ultimate sensual experience. All you need is baby oil or your favorite scented oil, a sheet of plastic, and a good sense of fun.

▲ **Once the scene is set, take off your clothes and sit facing each other, in the center of the plastic sheet. Pour a generous amount of oil into each of your hands and begin.**

$\mathscr{I}$magine your favorite scent – sweet warm vanilla or fresh tangy lemon; the rich texture of oil on your skin; the feel of your lover's hands gliding firmly down your back. Such is the pleasure of sensual massage.

In addition to its therapeutic value, massage is a tremendous turn-on. The masseur or masseuse can explore every inch of their partner's naked body, examining the different textures of skin and gentle undulations of form with their fingertips, while they watch them writhe with pleasure.

But often the idea of such a massage backfires, and your partner ends up wonderfully relaxed, blissfully satisfied – and asleep. Massage is such a gentle, soothing activity that it's hardly surprising that sleep is the result, although it is unfortunate for the other partner who has just dedicated an hour to caressing and stroking, and is now ready for something more.

READY FOR ACTION

To make the most of a sensual massage, and be sure of a climactic result, you need to make it more active. And in order to make it more active, you need more oil, more space and a few simple props.

Active massage tends to make more of a mess than a standard massage, where you can get away with no more than a large towel for protection. To prevent any seepage and stains, and make it more fun, you will need some towels and a large sheet of polythene. Clear a space in the middle of the bedroom or living room, and lay towels two or three

deep in that space. Then lay the plastic on top of the towels and weight the edges with furniture or heavy books. If you don't have a sheet of plastic, join

▼ *Smooth the oil into each other's skin, gliding your hands over the curves of their body. Gentle massage is an ideal way to get in the mood for a long session of sensuous lovemaking.*

DOS AND DON'TS

DO CHECK BY DOING A PATCH TEST THAT NEITHER OF YOU IS ALLERGIC TO THE OIL OR LOTION. CERTAIN AROMATHERAPY OILS CAN CAUSE A MILD IRRITATION TO SOME SKIN

DON'T ALLOW THE OIL TO COME INTO DIRECT CONTACT WITH THE SENSITIVE SKIN OF THE GENITALS. IF IT DOES, AND IT STARTS TO STING, WASH IT OFF IMMEDIATELY WITH A MILD SOAP AND WARM WATER

DON'T ALLOW THE OIL OR LOTION TO COME INTO CONTACT WITH A CONDOM. IT CAN ROT THE RUBBER AND REDUCE ITS CONTRACEPTIVE EFFECTIVENESS.

◀ **With your bodies covered in oil, you'll be able to move against each other in new ways, and create a rhythm and flow in your lovemaking.**

▼ *Turn your partner over and massage their buttocks and their inner thighs, then slide your body over the length of theirs. Let some oil spill on to the plastic and roll in to it. Then make love on the slippery surface.*

several strong garbage bags with tape, making sure there are no gaps.

SLOW START

Now that you are ready to begin, start with each other's neck, rubbing the oil around the front and back, then move on to the shoulders and upper arms. Any other part of the body is out of bounds while you work away the stress in the muscles. Spend at least five minutes on this area, particularly the neck and hairline, as this is one of the great erogenous zones.

When you are both satisfied, one of you can turn around and sit between the other's legs. While one partner works on the other's back, the other can work on the feet. Be generous with the oil. Cover the back and rub it all over. Smother the feet and calves, working between the toes and round the ankles.

When the skin is glistening and the muscles refreshed, you can have access to the rest of the body. Use plenty of oil – spread it liberally over the chest and breasts. Warm it first in your hands or

drizzle it straight from the bottle. Don't restrict the massage to your hands. You can now move every part of your oiled body against your partner's.   ❤

WRESTLING

Become sparring partners for a night and wrestle your way into your partner's heart – and bed – with a stimulating and energetic session in the ring. Guaranteed to make your heart beat faster and get your lovemaking started with a bang!

▼ *Seconds out – round one! Get ready for some fast-paced foreplay!*

The exciting sensation of physical closeness and skin-to-skin contact can make wrestling with your partner a thrilling and titillating experience – an altogether carnal prelude to lovemaking. As you engage in mock battle, your heart will begin to beat faster, your breath will come heavier, and your whole mind will be thrown into intense concentration on your own and your partner's body.

Many couples find that they make love more passionately after they have had a verbal argument. A wrestling match can provide a safe and exciting arena in which to struggle against each other, taking the battle between the sexes into the physical realm and making the final coming together that much more intense. But remember, this is a light-hearted and playful game for two caring people – do not play if you are

WHY NOT...

• WRESTLE NAKED AS A FUN VARIATION ON THE THEME.

• OPT FOR A SESSION IN THE RING WEARING A SIMPLE G-STRING AND BOOTS ONLY. LEATHER-WEAR LENDS A VERY SEXY, CARNAL TOUCH TO THE PROCEEDINGS.

• INCORPORATE AN S & M FEEL BY WEARING DOG COLLARS AND STUDDED BELTS.

really angry with your partner as things may potentially get out of hand. Make sure you follow certain rules to ensure nobody gets hurt:

• Don't pull limbs backwards so hard that you hurt your partner. You may not realize your own strength!

• Don't knee your partner in the groin. This can cause serious injury and not a little resentment.

• Don't stand on your lover's face or chest, even as a joke.

READY SET GO!

First of all, set up a mock ring in your living room or bedroom. Place a rubber sheet on the floor to mark the wrestling arena and to protect the rug from damage. Be sure to clear away all lamps and other breakable, fragile items so that you will feel free to grapple and wrangle to your heart's content. If you have a secluded garden, you may want to play outside.

Make sure that you both dress the part. Put on your sexiest and most alluring gym clothes. Women should wear a tight, low-cut Lycra body suit slit in a 'V' right down to the waist. As you bounce

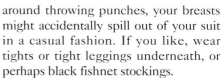

▲ *Tight, revealing clothes make the game more exciting, and give you something to grab hold of. Alternatively, why not try wrestling in the nude?*

▼ *It may not be an orthodox wrestling move, but it gives a whole new meaning to the term 'love bite!'*

around throwing punches, your breasts might accidentally spill out of your suit in a casual fashion. If you like, wear tights or tight leggings underneath, or perhaps black fishnet stockings.

Men should don sexy silky boxer shorts and a tight fitting tank top, or alternatively go bare from the waist up, depending on how good they feel about displaying their chests. Wear boots laced up high or go bare footed. The idea is to wear clothes which you know turn your partner on.

TOUCH DOWN 1-2-3

Ring a bell to indicate the start and end of the match. Decide the timing and the rules for each round. You may want to play some fast-paced music or play a sound-effects record or CD with crowd noises. The roar of the crowd will give you the kinky feeling of being watched as you fight and egg you on to greater heights of glory.

Try a few simple moves at first. Hop around and move in and out of your partner's space. Play a teasing game of coming up close, almost touching, and then moving away. You can use your hands to block and touch, grab and probe your partner. Real wrestling is sometimes just a show, with the moves decided beforehand. You can put on a

show of bravado and make mocking boasts just like the wrestlers you see on television.

BRAZEN MOVES
Now get down to business and lock arms as you push and swerve with each other. Get yourselves in a head-butt situation and try to outwit your lover into being the first one to make a false move. Pull him or her to the side and gently force them down on the mat. Slither your chest against theirs and get as close as you dare.

As you roll around, make sure you make plenty of skin contact. You could try wedging your leg in between your partner's, then flip them from side to side. Be rough, but not so rough that you are in any danger of hurting them. The trick is to be physical but not to go too far. For the finale, whoever is declared victor could move up and down over the vanquished in mock intercourse. You will soon be eager and ready for the real thing.

COOL CLIMAX
At the end of the match, be sure to sponge your partner's body from head to foot. Take a cloth or a big soft sponge dipped in cool water which has been scented with a drop or two of essential

▲ *Wrestling is perfect for women who prefer to take the dominant role in a sexual relationship, and is highly arousing for the passive man.*

▼ *The fun really starts at the end of the match, when the winner gets to claim their reward and the loser can look forward to being consoled in their defeat in the best way possible!*

oil. Sensuously pat it across your lover's forehead and cheeks, and across their neck and shoulders. At this point you may want to start removing each other's clothes and sponging down breasts, chest and legs. Leave the best bits for last and enjoy. Then you can squirm around together on the rubber mat, oiled and ready for further love play.

DARING ENCORE
Alternatively, both partners may want to jump under the shower while still wearing their wrestling gear. You can lather your lover all over with soap and shampoo. Rub the soap firmly and seductively in between their skin and wet clothing. Soak their hair and entire body. Make sure they are good and sudsy! Now pull your partner out of the shower and jump back in the ring, wet and soapy, only this time go straight to the rubber mat on the floor.

You could have a contest to see who can wrestle the other out of their clothes the quickest. The slippery struggle will make your touches even more titillating. The prize, a night of uninhibited lovemaking, ensures that everyone's a winner. ❤

BREAKFAST IN BED

Your budget may not run to caviar and champagne, but there is nothing to stop you celebrating Sunday in bed with a sumptuous banquet of food and sex.

There are few simple pleasures greater than a lazy Sunday spent in bed with your partner. But busy lives make such lounging a luxury. Whether your peace is shattered by children, unsocial working hours or separate weekend pursuits, the mornings you can call your own are rare. So to make the most of your time together, tease your partner from the depths of slumber with a breakfast banquet in bed.

HUNGRY FOR LOVE

Early-morning lovemaking can create incredible appetites, and if you want to

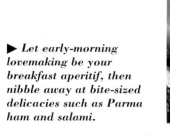

▲ *Turn your breakfast into a sensual feast by feeding each other aphrodisiacs, such as asparagus.*

▶ *Let early-morning lovemaking be your breakfast aperitif, then nibble away at bite-sized delicacies such as Parma ham and salami.*

◀ With their soft fleshy skin and sweetly oozing juices, peaches or nectarines are an obvious choice for any sensual feast.

▶ Make kissing an even sweeter experience with fresh fruits, such as strawberries, cherries and blueberries.

▼ Refreshing and instantly edible, grapes will add zest to your early-morning lovemaking.

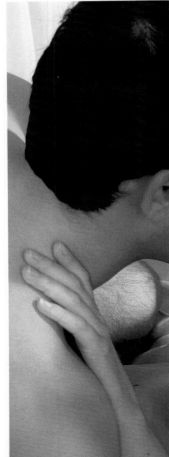

maintain your partner's sexual strength you need a satisfying and inspiring breakfast to share.

Whatever your preference for a morning meal, make it bite sized and instantly edible. And choose food which will give you energy, rather than send you back to sleep again.

As it's more likely to be brunch than breakfast, finely cut cold meats, like honey roast ham, Parma ham and turkey, make great appetizers. Served with chilled melon, olives or rye bread, they make a wonderful start to the day.

SUGGESTIVE DELIGHTS

Select your food for the look as much as the taste. Asparagus is a traditional aphrodisiac, but gained its reputation possibly more for the phallic shape than any magical properties. Cooked in advance and arranged individually on plates, together with two cherry tomatoes and a large sprig of parsley, they

may just amuse and excite enough to have a positive effect on your partner's libido.

FOOD, GLORIOUS FOOD

Hot coffee, tea, freshly squeezed orange juice, smoked salmon and scrambled eggs, and a Mimosa, can turn breakfast into a leisurely feast.

And bear in mind that the food you prepare need not necessarily be just for eating. Not only can you titillate by suggestive presentation, but you can use each dish as a prelude to yet more love-making.

If you have yogurt on the menu, don't restrict it to the dish. It is the perfect natural accompaniment to oral sex. Grab a towel from the bathroom to save the sheets, then pour, spoon or finger the yogurt over your partner's genitals. Hold them while they squeal in response to the cool and creamy liquid, then slowly and meticulously lick the yogurt off their body. Bon appetit! ♥

WHY NOT...

• POP A BUNCH OF SWEET, SEEDLESS GRAPES IN THE FREEZER BEFORE YOU GO TO BED. IN THE MORNING THEY WILL TASTE LIKE A DELICIOUSLY REFRESHING GRAPE SORBET. TREAT THEM LIKE ICE CUBES – PLACE ONE IN THE NAVEL AND LET IT MELT A LITTLE BEFORE SUCKING IT OUT. EAT A HANDFUL, THEN WITH AN ICE-COLD TONGUE KISS YOUR PARTNER'S GENITALS!

• SURPRISE YOUR PARTNER ON HIS OR HER BIRTHDAY OR YOUR ANNIVERSARY. BRING IN THE BANQUET ACCOMPANIED BY A BUNCH OF FRESH FLOWERS AND THE DAY WILL SLIP GLORIOUSLY AWAY.

• BLINDFOLD YOUR PARTNER AND LET THEM GUESS WHAT YOU'RE FEEDING THEM AS YOU PUT EACH NEW MORSEL INTO THEIR MOUTH.

STRIPTEASE

Anyone can undress in front of their partner, unless they are very inhibited, but few people fully realize the erotic potential of striptease as a prelude to lovemaking.

Striptease involves stripping off one's clothes and, in so doing, teasing one's audience. Here we are talking about the woman stripping for her man, but this is not a one-way street. The man will certainly enjoy himself, but the woman can also become aroused by her own sexually explicit behavior, as well as by the effect she is having.

PREPARE YOURSELF

Prepare the scene and yourself beforehand to ensure the best possible outcome. You could have a small drink to loosen up, then make sure the lighting is good and that you are not going to be interrupted. Choose some suitable music that lasts longer than the average three or four minutes, so that you have plenty of time to complete your strip. It should also have a strong beat.

DOWN TO BASICS

The basic principle of stripping is to save the best part – the tease – until last.

Start by putting on make-up, however much you think your partner would like, and do your hair, paint your nails, have a bath and so on.

Next, choose your clothes carefully. Avoid fidgety fastenings. Wear only a very few clothes and only those that can be easily removed. Your best choice would be a dress (or blouse and skirt), bra and panties, stockings and a garter belt, high heels and some jewelry.

Create the right atmosphere. Put on the music and settle your partner down.

◄ ▲ Take it slowly and seductively, moving in time to the music. Don't show too much too soon – remember that 'tease' is the name of the game.

Kiss and stroke him a little to get him excited and interested. After this, you are not going to touch him until the whole striptease is over, and you make love.

TEASING TIPS

• IF YOU'RE SHY, PRACTICE STRIPPING TO MUSIC ON YOUR OWN FIRST OF ALL. WHEN YOU'VE PERFECTED A ROUTINE, GIVE YOUR PARTNER A PLEASANT SURPRISE ONE NIGHT.

• ENHANCE YOUR OWN PLEASURE DURING THE STRIPTEASE WITH SOME ORIENTAL LOVE BALLS. THESE ARE SMALL HOLLOW PLASTIC SPHERES WITH A HEAVY BALL-BEARING INSIDE. YOU PUT THEM INTO YOUR VAGINA BEFORE YOU START TO STRIP. AS YOU MOVE AROUND TO THE MUSIC, THE BALLS MOVE INSIDE YOU, PRODUCING DELIGHTFUL, AROUSING SENSATIONS. DON'T FORGET TO TAKE THEM OUT BEFORE YOU MAKE LOVE!

• IN THE SUMMER, GO OUT SOMEWHERE FORMAL AND PUBLIC WITH SIMPLY A DRESS AND SHOES ON AND NOTHING UNDERNEATH. OPEN YOUR LEGS CASUALLY, AS YOU SIT OPPOSITE YOUR LOVER, SO HE ALONE CAN SEE UP YOUR SKIRT.

• TRY MAKING EVERYDAY UNDRESSING A BIT OF A TEASE TOO. JUST MAKE A LITTLE EFFORT TO REMOVE YOUR BRA SEXILY, OR MAKE A SHOW OF REMOVING YOUR PANTIES.

BRING ON THE DANCING GIRL

Start by dancing around to the music, as if you were dancing at a disco, but emphasize your breasts, legs and bottom. Run your hands down the outside of your hips and thighs, over your arms, and over your breasts. Run your fingers through your hair, and generally cover your body with strokes, as though it were your man doing it.

Slowly undo your blouse in a teasing way to reveal more of your breasts. When all the buttons are undone, turn around with your back to him, tease down the top of your blouse and remove it. Cover your breasts with it, and turn to him, so that it looks as though your top is naked beneath the crumpled blouse. Never remove any garment over your head – it rarely looks elegant and ruins your hairstyle. Now throw the blouse over to him, revealing your top half.

Undo the waistband of your skirt, and wriggle out of it, letting it fall to the ground. Step out of it, and kick it over to him. Do the wriggling out bit very slowly and seductively, teasing him as the skirt slips down your hips to reveal panties and garter belt. This can all be greatly enhanced by turning around and revealing your bottom as it emerges from the skirt. Next, take off your shoes slowly and sexily.

Sit on a high stool or chair and slowly undo your stockings from the garter belt, one at a time. Roll down one stocking at a time to the toe, and remove it sexily. Once you have removed your stockings, put your shoes back on – this enhances the shape of your legs. Now you are wearing only bra, panties, garter belt and shoes.

SAVING THE BEST FOR LAST

Stand up, and dance some more. Emphasize your breasts, because they are to be the next center of attraction. Remove one bra strap then the other, and with your back to your man, undo the clip behind. Hold your bra to your chest with your hands over both breasts, and turn around to face him. Now, to the music, do a peek-a-boo with first one breast and then the other. Finally, toss the bra over to him with a flourish.

Dance around now, shaking your breasts to the music. Go over to him, and tease him by holding your breasts very close to his face. But remember: no touching. If he tries, leap away.

Now go back to your dance position out of his reach, and slowly and sexily remove your panties. Turn with your back to him, and edge them down ever so gently in time to the music. Let them fall to the ground, when you are facing towards or away from him, whichever you know he prefers. Kick them over to him, or pick them up, and drape them over him.

Dance around now to the rhythm, then remove your garter belt or G-string, and display yourself really well. Stroke and caress yourself all over your body in time to the music.

Lie down on the floor, and writhe around to the music. Facing him, open up your legs and stroke your vulva. Lie

on your tummy then get on all fours, and caress your bottom so that you are totally open to his view. Lying on your back, caress your breasts and nipples. Wet a finger or two and moisten your nipples, then caress your clitoral area. From here on it is likely your partner will want to get in on the action as he will have been teased quite enough. ❤

▲ *With your back to your partner, slowly remove your panties, cheekily playing peek-a-boo. When the time is right you could turn around and drape your panties over your partner.*

STRIPTEASE – HIM FOR HER

Surprise your partner by tempting her with your own personal striptease act. And by daring to bear all, you can provide a tantalizing prelude to a sexy evening of naked fun.

With the onslaught of the Chippendales and other male acts geared towards sexually stimulating and pleasing women, the male striptease is alive and thriving – and not just in cabarets and clubs.

Stripping for your lover can be a wonderful way to boost her sexual interest and provide her with fantasy material for some time to come. You needn't have a perfect, glowing body to entertain her – just dim the lights and 'strut your stuff.' Remember, she probably has a good

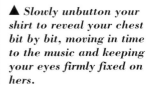

▲ *Slowly unbutton your shirt to reveal your chest bit by bit, moving in time to the music and keeping your eyes firmly fixed on hers.*

◄ *Move close to her and ask her to lick your bared chest. But just as her tongue darts from her lips, draw back smiling tantilizingly.*

77

imagination anyway, so be bold and confident and strip with style.

WHAT SHE WANTS

A woman usually craves a feeling of intimacy and closeness from the sexual side of her relationship. But occasionally, she will like to be taken by storm and charmed with a vision of illicit, passionate sex with a stranger. You can create this 'dangerous' atmosphere of altered sexuality by following a few easy guidelines.

You may want to surprise her with an impromptu striptease, or lead her on through the day with kinky little hints of what you have in mind. Set the mood with lighting and music, whatever type suits the sort of performance you wish to give. The beat can be slow and sexy, or it can be fast and passionate.

SUITS YOU

It is a good idea to start your striptease session fully clothed, and if possible, in your very best suit. This gives you many items of clothing to remove, and provides the sexy contrast between being formally dressed and seductively naked. Begin by throwing your keys and wallet on a chair with great abandon. Unbutton and pull your jacket off slowly, one arm and then the other. Wriggle out of it and

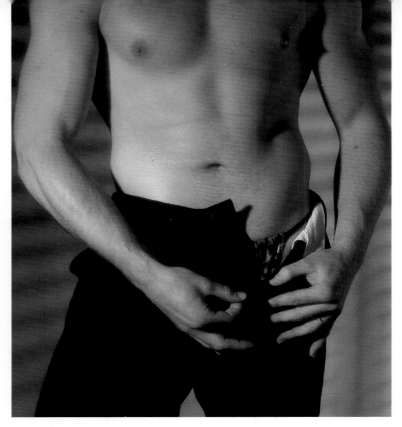

▲ *Playing with your genitals and pretending to masturbate while groaning with pleasure is certain to have her reaching out to do it for you. But don't let her. Remember, stripTEASE is the name of the game.*

WHY NOT...

• TAKE HER ON A COUNTRY HOLIDAY OR A WEEKEND BREAK AND SURPRISE HER WITH AN IMPROMPTU STRIP SESSION AS YOU GET READY TO SNUGGLE INTO BED.

• ASK YOUR LOVER TO JOIN IN THE FUN AND PLAY A DARING STRIP GAME WHERE YOU MUST EACH REMOVE AN ITEM OF CLOTHING IN TURN.

• SHOUT 'HONEY, I'M HOME!' AS YOU WALK THROUGH THE DOOR FROM WORK. BEGIN BY REMOVING YOUR COAT AS USUAL. THEN, CASUALLY KEEP GOING AS THOUGH IT IS PERFECTLY NORMAL FOR YOU TO TAKE OFF ALL YOUR CLOTHES IN THE KITCHEN OR HALLWAY. YOU CAN MAKE LOVE IN ANY ROOM OF THE HOUSE.

throw it behind you nonchalantly.

Now loosen your tie. Make a show of pulling it off and twisting it around your lover's waist or lightly whipping her with it. Be sure to keep up good eye contact with her throughout. Slowly unbutton your shirt, moving to the beat of the music. Don't worry if you are not a good dancer – just follow your instincts. As you remove your shirt, move your chest close to her face and ask her to lick it. When her tongue has nearly touched your skin, pull away teasingly.

THE BOTTOM LINE

You can have a lot of fun from the waist down. First, bend over with your backside facing her and take off your shoes – you may want to let her help you unlace them – then remove your socks. Unbuckle your belt and pull it quickly from your waist. Whip it into the air, perhaps jumping over it as you flick it

across the floor. Now smoothly rub your hands over your chest and down towards your crotch. Insert one hand into the waist of your trousers and simulate masturbation.

BE A TEASE

Move teasingly close to her after you have unzipped your fly. She may wish to reach out to you at this point, but tell her that she can look but not touch until you give the go-ahead. Dance seductively out of your trousers to reveal the skimpy G-string you are wearing underneath. Now is the time to let her experience her desire fully. Let her fondle your genitals for a while before pulling away and removing your G-string. ❤

▲ *Gyrate your hips to show off what's in your G-string. Now she can caress you with her hands and even lick your G-string, but keep it on for a minute or two longer and she will be in a frenzy of sexual anticipation.*

▶ *Step out of the G-string and let her run her hands all over your body. You've been doing all the work so far, now it's her turn. You will both be so turned on by now that a memorable bout of love-making lies in store for both of you.*

3

Role Playing

Sexual fantasies, rather than being repressed, should be developed to enhance your love life, providing an aura of excitement and a taste of the forbidden. The scenarios given here will allow you to forget yourselves and adopt new, erotic personas that permit you to behave as never before. With different acts in which each partner can tease and dominate, you will soon find yourselves surrendering to temptation.

FUN WITH ROLE-PLAYING

We all wish we were someone else from time to time – and sometimes we wish our partners were someone else – especially in bed. Role-playing games can be a tremendously creative and exciting way to spice up your love life without actually resorting to having an affair with someone else.

▲ *Back to the schoolroom. Only this time, the lessons you and your lover are about to learn are somewhat hotter and a lot more fun!*

For the creative couple, role-playing adds enjoyment to their lives just as other hobbies do. Most couples play these games simply for the sheer fun of them. With a little imagination, they will enable you to come up with cheeky, fresh ideas for loving foreplay and they will add exciting new twists to your usual favorite lovemaking techniques.

AUDITION YOUR FANTASY

You can explore your secret fantasies and provocative sensual whims, then act them out with the thought that you will become a completely different character every time. Since you are playing a part, and are not restricted to your own personality traits or usual habits, you will have the thrilling freedom of being able to say and do things that you would not normally do during your lovemaking activities.

But role-playing games need not be restricted to the bedroom at night – you may want to assume these characters earlier in the day for a teasing and tantalizing build-up.

ROLE CALL

In whatever game you choose, one partner must take the lead or dominant role, and the other person takes the passive, submissive role. Whether you are playing principal and school boy, mother and baby, doctor and nurse, or one of the many other variations, the key is to transform yourself and your lover from your everyday personae.

WHAT'S UP, DOC?

Doctors 'tell' people to undress and display their private body parts and this is why 'doctors and nurses' is such a popular game in childhood. For many couples the same game is arousing right up to adulthood – it is popular especially with women. A game that 'compels' her to act sexually becomes exciting because it absolves her from any anxiety or guilt she may have in enjoying herself. She can give herself over freely and wholly to lovemaking because she is being 'forced' – in this case for her own good – by a medical man.

Similarly, a man may enjoy being told what to do by a strict nurse. He may enjoy the thrill of being dominated by a woman. Most men are very aroused when a woman takes the initiative in

sex, and this can be played out in many ways. The Patient enters the room fully dressed and then the Doctor or Nurse tells them that they will require a full examination and must remove all of their clothes. The sight of one person stripping while the other remains fully clothed can be highly arousing in itself. The Doctor or Nurse then orders the Patient onto the table for an intimate 'examination' of the genitals including long, internal examinations of the woman about which the Doctor then comments in detail.

YES, M'LADY

The sexual liaison of the lady of the house with her chauffeur, gardener or other servant has always been a popular theme. *Lady Chatterley's Lover* shocked the world when it was first published with its explicit sexual detail of the affair of the sex-starved Lady Chatterley and

▶ *An aerobics class with a difference. As the sweat builds up, the Teacher may become a little too friendly and show the Student the moves, touching him or her more and more intimately.*

▼ *Before you start your role-playing game decide between you who is going to be the seducer and who is going to be seduced. Then, get into your roles and let your new 'characters' set the pace!*

the natural juices already flowing, is bound to make you both eager for a little 'extra-curricular' activity.

ENCORE

Once you find a game you both enjoy, add other stimulating elements so that your enjoyment of it is heightened. You can use your intuition to try and guess which new roles will turn your lover on, and surprise them by launching into the role when they least expect it. Let your natural instincts run wild. ❤

her earthy, sensual gardener. The gardener eventually breaks down the reserve of the repressed upper class lady, and instructs her in the practices of the sensual world about which she at first knows little.

Lady Chatterley and her gardener were often to be found engaged in embraces outdoors in the woods and fields. They had special pet names for their genitals and other body parts, and often wove wild flowers into their pubic hair as they spent long, lingering, sunny afternoons making love in the open air.

STRUT THAT STUFF

Many people have had crushes on their teachers as children, being naturally attracted to those more sexually and emotionally developed. You can play out this type of fantasy by re-creating a gym class in your living room. One person takes the lead as the Teacher, the other the enthused, adoring Student.

Both partners should don tight, revealing gym clothes. The Teacher can then put an aerobics video on the video recorder, or simply play some fast-paced music and begin the work-out by calling out the exercises.

He may then comment on the heat in the room, as he nonchalantly starts to strip off his tight, lycra clothing. This display of exhibitionism, combined with

◀▼ While you may have trouble finding remote locations for your own love play, you can use the Lady/Gardener theme just as well at home. The Gardener struts bullishly into the room from the 'grounds' while the Lady wearing prim, old-fashioned clothes, waits to be seduced, undressed and 'taught' about sex for the first time. She may act unwilling at the start, but she soon begins to understand and lets her natural instincts take over with a passion she never thought possible.

NURSE, NURSE!

We all like to feel pampered and cared for when we are sick – it can be a real turn-on to have a nurse tend to our every need. You can re-enact a sick bed scene with a sexy twist and let nurse kiss it better for a night of patient passion.

Being completely at the mercy of a sexy nurse could make for a fabulous fantasy for many men. But fortunately you don't have to wait until you are ill to enjoy it. Why not recreate a 'make-believe' hospital scene at home, where the man is the patient and the woman the pert nurse, ready to tend to his every need with loving care.

SETTING THE SCENE

You can set up your own bed, or even use the dining room table as a hospital bed. Cover it with lots of blankets and comfortable pillows and hang a sheet round it on wooden poles for an

▲ *The kinky nurse look is deceptively simple – just don a suitable dress or apron and an improvised hat and prepare for some health care with a difference!*

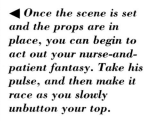

◀ *Once the scene is set and the props are in place, you can begin to act out your nurse-and-patient fantasy. Take his pulse, and then make it race as you slowly unbutton your top.*

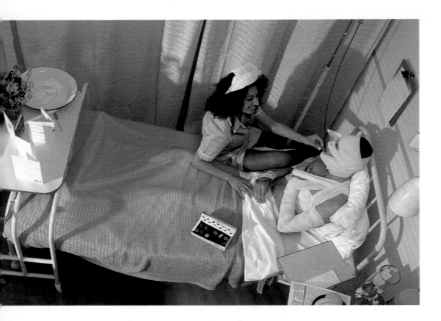

up in band aids and bandages. The sight of a sick, bed-ridden person can excite tender, protective feelings in a woman, which may lead to greater closeness when the bandages come off. You can use bits of cotton sheeting torn into strips, or to be really sensual, use strips of silk or silky scarves. This will give the impression of his being at your mercy without entering the realms of heavy bondage. He will probably be very aroused by the idea of your taking charge and giving him orders.

CARING SHARING

Take your time and slowly wrap his head very loosely leaving eye, nose and mouth openings, massaging the back of his neck with your fingers. Next wrap his chest, seductively rubbing your cheek and lips against it as you go, then perhaps wrap one of his legs, kissing and licking the pretend wounds. If you want to get really silly, you can turn your love play into a comedy/horror extravaganza that will leave you both giggling, cuddling and screaming with laughter. Wind bandages round every part of his body, except for his neck, so that he

authentic hospital feel. The nurse can improvise the 'uniform,' by wearing an apron over a simple dress. Her hat can be made out of a white paper napkin. For the simplest scenario the patient need only wear a pair of pyjamas.

The extent of the drama is really up to you. Why not indulge in some bandage bondage – go wild and cover him

▲ *Hitch up your 'uniform' and indulge in some passion with your patient.*

▼ *As his temperature rises, why not join him in bed and cool him down with a soothing sponge bath.*

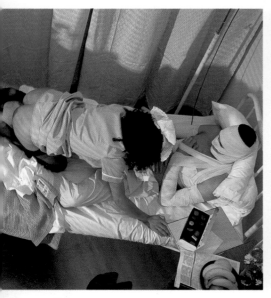

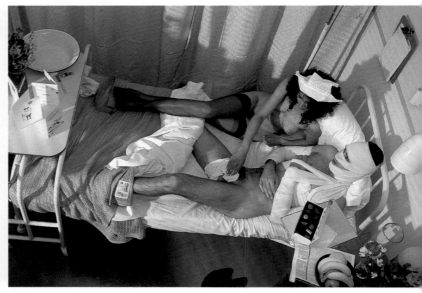

WHY NOT...

• SWAP ROLES AND LET THE WOMAN BE THE PATIENT TENDED TO AND THE MAN A MALE NURSE. INSTEAD OF SWATHING HER IN BANDAGES, GIVE HER A COMPLETE CHECK UP BEFORE PROCEEDING WITH SEXUAL HEALING.

• PRETEND YOU ARE IN A TELEVISION MEDICAL SOAP OPERA OR DRAMA SERIAL AND PLAY YOUR FAVORITE CHARACTERS, PERHAPS ENDING UP IN THE BROOM CUPBOARD FOR A QUICKIE.

looks like a mummy or the invisible man. Wrap each part seductively, slowly tickling his skin with your nails as you bind him.

SPONGE BATH

Nurse may begin by giving the patient a sponge bath, patting her warm wet sponge seductively against his chest and arms. If she is feeling wicked, she may dip the sponge in cold water and dab it lightly along his inner thighs. As he squeals with chilly delight, she may be so overcome by her compassion for him that she simply must join him in bed.

Perhaps she will guide his hand up under her uniform, whereupon he quickly discovers that she has forgotten to wear her regulation white stockings and panties. Despite his 'illness,' he may just feel strong enough to beckon her to get on top of him for some special private medical care.

KISS AND TOUCH

To show his appreciation, the patient may feel obliged to kiss and touch her with his unbandaged mouth. But first he must pull her uniform off completely so that she can feel the full force of his gratitude. Then she can settle back gently and fondle his poor bandaged head

▲ *Pamper your patient by pandering to his every need – sexual and otherwise.*

▼ *He might want to show his gratitude for your 'hands-on' approach to nursing by indulging in a spot of oral sex.*

as he gives her a spot of healthy oral sex. This will be extremely exciting for her as she can fantasize and pretend he is one of her heroes – perhaps her favorite film or pop star – in his bandaged disguise.

INTENSIVE CARE

To make his stay in the hospital memorable enjoy some passionate, deep penetration lovemaking in a bed-rocking finale. Later on, if you are both still in the mood, swap roles and start again! ♥

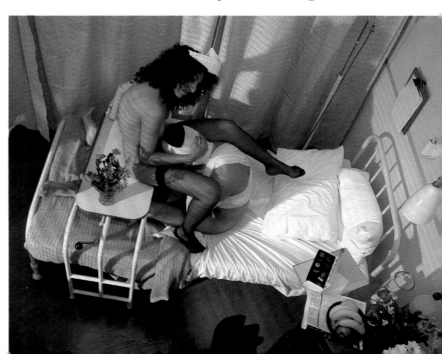

THROUGH THE WINDOW

Surprise your partner while he is working and indulge in a little classic fantasy, with one as the handsome young window cleaner and the other as the sexy temptress.

Spontaneity is one of the great factors cited as the key to a successful sexual relationship. So what better way to turn your partner on than surprising them with a treat when he or she least expects it? As so much of our spare time is taken up with mundane but necessary tasks, why not use these dull occasions to delight your loved one with a touch of traditional fantasy?

TEDIOUS TASKS

One of the worst jobs around the home is window cleaning, yet it can have certain benefits that many people have never considered. The British comic George Formby touched upon it in his

▲ *If your partner has agreed to clean the windows, why not have a surprise waiting for him when he works his way round to the bedroom?*

▶ *Wearing your sexiest underwear, now is the time to practice your striptease skills – remember 'teasing' is the name of the game.*

classic ditty *When I'm Cleaning Windows*, a song which describes all the funny and bizarre antics people get up to while he is busy carrying out his job. Of course, although no respectable professional would ever dream of spying on his customers, it is quite a different matter when looking through the windows of your own home.

SETTING THE SCENE

Your partner may regularly clean and polish the windows. Or he or she may have to be coaxed and cajoled into it when they are so filthy you can no longer see through them. Either way, you will get a certain amount of advance warning to plan the scenario (if he is cleaning the windows you can opt for the strategy below; and if she is cleaning the windows you will have to adapt the seduction scene with a Chippendales-style performance to suit her).

SEDUCTION TRICKS

As soon as he steps outside with his bucket and his sponge, you have to be prepared to spring into action. Take a quick shower or bath, cover yourself with fra-

▲▲ *This should do it. Whatever stage he is at with his window cleaning chores, he will be dashing into your arms to sample the delights that have been so seductively displayed.*

▼ *He may want to make love immediately, but make sure your steamy session cannot be seen from outside!*

grant body lotion or perfume, then change into the sexiest underwear you can find. Top the outfit with a slinky silken robe or similar in order to look as seductive as possible.

Before he begins to clean the windows of your planned room, draw the curtains or blinds so that he cannot see inside. Then, once he is on the final polish, pull them open to reveal a vision of yourself, at your dressing table combing your hair, sipping a glass of wine in the dining room,

or even with a tray of coffee and cookies in the kitchen or living room.

Once he has recovered himself, move towards the window and start to coax him inside. If the windows are still closed, he won't be able to hear you until you deign to open them, so you will have to encourage him with your actions.

Carry on with your chosen activity – brushing your hair, pouring coffee, sipping your wine or reading a magazine. Then let your robe fall away slightly,

▲ ▲ *As long as you are sure of your privacy, take your time to indulge in some oral sex – you for him, and him for you.*

▼ *Make passionate love below the window he has so carefully cleaned, and you ensure that you will never view cleaning windows in the same way again!*

revealing your underwear beneath. Stand up and walk around, letting the robe slip slinkily away. You could pretend to have dropped something, bending over to give him a really good view of your buttocks.

If he is showing signs that he cannot wait for you any longer, open the window and haul him in. And now is the time to put your striptease skills into action. One thing is for certain, cleaning the windows will never be the same dull household chore again! ❤

DOS AND DON'TS

• DON'T PUT ON A FLOOR SHOW FOR THE NEIGHBORS.

• DO WANDER AROUND THE OUTSIDE OF YOUR HOUSE BEFORE YOU BEGIN TO CHECK OUT THE SCENE OF SEDUCTION.

• DO MAKE SURE THAT, ONCE THROUGH THE WINDOW, YOU REMAIN SEDUCTIVELY HIDDEN FROM PRYING EYES. YOU CAN EITHER CARRY ON YOUR STEAMY SESSION ON THE FLOOR – OR DRAW THE CURTAINS.

ARTIST AND MODEL

You don't have to be a great artist to paint your partner; all you need is a strong and creative passion for the physical body – and the rest can be up to you both!

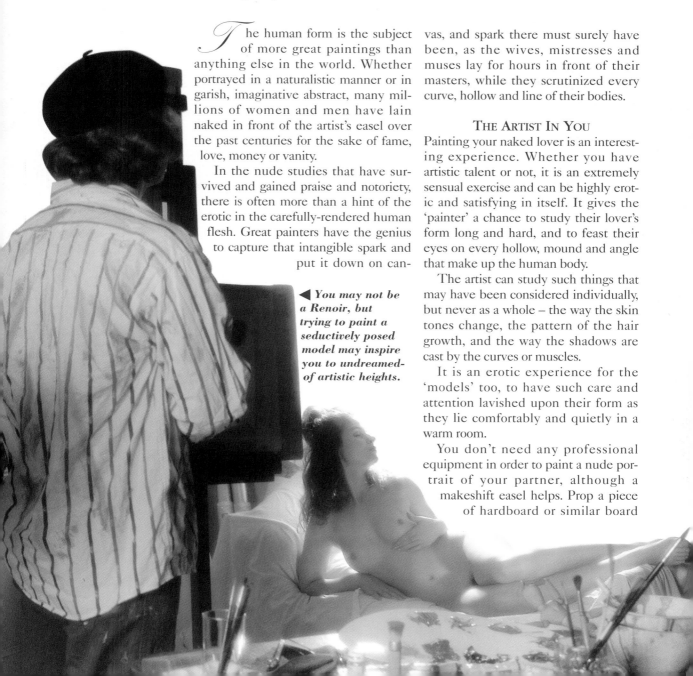

The human form is the subject of more great paintings than anything else in the world. Whether portrayed in a naturalistic manner or in garish, imaginative abstract, many millions of women and men have lain naked in front of the artist's easel over the past centuries for the sake of fame, love, money or vanity.

In the nude studies that have survived and gained praise and notoriety, there is often more than a hint of the erotic in the carefully-rendered human flesh. Great painters have the genius to capture that intangible spark and put it down on can-

◄ You may not be a Renoir, but trying to paint a seductively posed model may inspire you to undreamed- of artistic heights.

vas, and spark there must surely have been, as the wives, mistresses and muses lay for hours in front of their masters, while they scrutinized every curve, hollow and line of their bodies.

THE ARTIST IN YOU

Painting your naked lover is an interesting experience. Whether you have artistic talent or not, it is an extremely sensual exercise and can be highly erotic and satisfying in itself. It gives the 'painter' a chance to study their lover's form long and hard, and to feast their eyes on every hollow, mound and angle that make up the human body.

The artist can study such things that may have been considered individually, but never as a whole – the way the skin tones change, the pattern of the hair growth, and the way the shadows are cast by the curves or muscles.

It is an erotic experience for the 'models' too, to have such care and attention lavished upon their form as they lie comfortably and quietly in a warm room.

You don't need any professional equipment in order to paint a nude portrait of your partner, although a makeshift easel helps. Prop a piece of hardboard or similar board against a solid object, making sure there is enough space for you to move around behind it and see your partner fully.

If you don't have large sheets of sketching paper, the back of an old roll of wallpaper will do, so long as it is smooth. The expanse of paper will give

▲ *Painting your naked partner is such a sensual experience that even before the paint has dried on the board, you may be tempted to succumb, like countless artists before you, to the beguiling charms of your model.*

WHY NOT...

FOR THE SERIOUSLY ARTISTIC, BODY PRINTING MAKES FOR A GREAT EVENING'S ENTERTAINMENT. MIX SOME NON-TOXIC WATER-BASED PAINT TO THE CONSISTENCY OF THICK CREAM, THEN LAY A LARGE SHEET OF PLASTIC ON THE FLOOR. COVER THE PLASTIC WITH SHEETS OF WALLPAPER, WRONG SIDE UP, OR LARGE SHEETS OF PAPER, THEN BEGIN!

COVER PARTS OF YOUR BODY WITH THE STICKY PAINT – BREASTS, PALMS, BUTTOCKS AND FEET – THEN PRESS THEM ON THE PAPER TO CREATE A FABULOUS BODY PRINT. MAKE IT AS ABSTRACT OR REALISTIC AS YOU LIKE – YOU COULD EVEN TRY MAKING YOUR OWN FULL-FRONTAL ABSTRACT ON A SHEET BY COVERING THE WHOLE LENGTH OF YOUR BODY WITH PAINT AND GETTING YOUR PARTNER TO PRESS THE SHEET OVER YOU. PART OF THE FUN WILL BE SHOWERING EACH OTHER CLEAN AT THE END OF THE GAME.

▲ *It probably won't be long before you, too, are naked and letting your sensitive hands pleasure the parts of your partners body that you were so recently committing to canvas.*

▶ *Your painting may not match a Manet, but the lovemaking that your artistic efforts leads to is sure to make you want to try your hand at it again and again...*

you plenty of room for making sketches.

You can choose any medium you like to work in – charcoal, poster paints, pastels – but remember whatever you choose will dictate the style of the final outcome. With brightly colored kids' paints, you can go for an abstract, pop-art style of figure, with pencil or pen a simple sketch, with oils a more traditional style of painting.

GETTING STARTED

Set up your equipment, then, making sure the room is warm enough for your partner to sit nude, work on the pose. It must be comfortable if it is to be held for more than five minutes, so reclining on a bed or sofa is perhaps the one to go for. Cover the surface he or she is to lie on with a dust sheet so the background is not a distraction, then start experimenting with positions.

You may have a firm idea of what you want, in which case try it and see if it works. Otherwise sit at your easel and let your partner experiment him- or herself until you spot something that looks right. A Polaroid camera will help at this stage, as a snap can always be referred to

for positioning if the model needs to stretch during the session.

Begin with bold, wild strokes to capture the curves, lines and planes. You will be looking at your partner in a new way, and may well discover aspects of them which seem unfamiliar – a mole here, a patch of darker skin there – it's not a question of having been inattentive before, just that now you are forced to look at every inch and reproduce it on paper.

If at first the sketch doesn't please, try again. You will soon learn to transform the lines of reality to lines on paper. You might be surprised at your early prowess. As soon as you arrive at a sketch you are happy with, you can start to paint. As your colors start to bring the picture to life, your passion will begin to rise. The delicate bloom of the skin, the smooth tautness of the muscles or the dark shock of pubic hair might just be enough to distract you from your work of art.

Give in to the urge, as artists are entitled to be wild and impetuous, and make dirty, painty love to your muse on the studio floor. ❤

DIRTY DANCING

Try the tango when you're alone with your partner. You may find yourselves taken totally unawares at just how far the rhythm takes you.

It has been said that the tango is the vertical expression of a horizontal desire. Performed well, it is certainly the sexiest, most evocative dance imaginable.

The origins of this slow, sensuous dance are steeped in mystery. It is claimed that it traveled from Central Africa with the African slaves to South America where it was adopted by the hot-blooded Argentinians. They gave it a flavor all of their own, taking in evocative foreign influences such as the Cuban Habenera.

The tango evolved, not in the sophisticated dance halls where the rich gathered, but in city streets, where the impoverished lower classes used it as an abandoned form of self-expression and entertainment, giving it all the fire, violence and passion mirrored by their own hard lives.

When it appeared in the society ballrooms in the early years of the 20th century, many people were shocked by the dance and labeled it a public disgrace. Prudish matrons were offended most by the smouldering sexuality of the 'Gypsy' dancers who demonstrated it. Their horrified eyes took in the thrusting, pulsating movements of each couple, decked in their glittering costumes.

▶ **Who knows where it will end as you give yourselves up to the tantalizing tempo of the tango?**

◀ **He whirls her into position, his hand pressed into the small of her back, their bodies thigh to thigh, groin to groin.**

94

◄ His hand pulls her closer: her hands ensure that there will soon be little between them.

▼ The music pulsates on, provoking you both to forsake any pretense of self-control.

► You spin around each other until you reach a position that you know from experience is mutually satisfying. And as the music comes to its thrilling climax, so, too, do you in a cocktail of tango and sex.

Unlike all the other sexy, suggestive dances that have thrilled and horrified audiences, the tango retains a dignity which allies it more to the sexual act than any other dance.

Public performance of the modern tango is carefully choreographed. Your private performance needn't be. It is as much about doing what you feel as following the rules. Try it for fun with your partner – and don't be afraid to go where the rhythm leads you.

IN THE MOOD

First you need to get some of the spirit of the tango into your blood. Put on some tango music. Then draw the curtains, turn down the lights, turn up the volume, and let the wild melody course through your veins.

In the land of your imagination there

her on to the tiny dance floor. He whirls her into position, his hand pressed tight in the small of her back to lock their bodies together. The dance continues, becoming ever more sexual in its movements, the dancers' concentrated expressions giving out a passion that starts to work the crowd into a frenzy.

Now there is no one else on the dance floor but the two of them, and a hush has fallen over the heaving crowd which watches, mesmerized, as the dancers gyrate to their spectacular climax. In the gloom of the bar they could almost be making love in time to the cheers of the crowd on the dance floor.

BACK TO REALITY

Once aroused by the image of your tango fantasy, coax your partner out of his or her seat – change the music if necessary, putting on something with a more familiar, modern beat. Hold him tight against you, and start to move, thinking of the dance more as choreographed sex in an upright position.

When you can wait no more, make passionate love. The athletic can try it in the dance position, standing up, or the man can sweep her up into his arms and take her to the bed or sofa. Keep up the rhythm of the dance, and have sex in time to the music. ❤

are two people – your alter egos. It is a sticky, humid night in a poor South American town and they are sitting in the corner of a crowded, noisy bar, drinking ice-cold margaritas to quench their thirsts in the heat of the tropical night. She is wearing a red silk dress, cut to reveal her shapely, athletic figure, and he is wearing simple black trousers and a black silk shirt, worn loose and partly open, showing a muscular, tanned chest. As the band strikes up the familiar chords of the tango, he leaps to his feet, catching her around the waist and spinning

WHY NOT...

• WATCH FILMS TO INSPIRE YOU – PATRICK SWAYZE'S *DIRTY DANCING* CAN BE VERY INSPIRATIONAL.

• DRESS FOR THE OCCASION. HE SHOULD WEAR A SILK SHIRT AND BUTTOCK-HUGGING TROUSERS. SHE SHOULD WEAR A FLUID, SEXY SLIT SKIRT AND A LOW-CUT, HIGHLY REVEALING TOP. TRY IT WITHOUT ANY UNDERWEAR: BUT KEEP THAT A SECRET!

• DANCE IN FRONT OF A FULL-LENGTH MIRROR LIKE PROFESSIONALS, BUT IF THE SIGHT OF YOURSELVES CAVORTING AROUND IS TOO MUCH, AT LEAST YOU CAN LAUGH BEFORE YOUR LOVEMAKING.

MAID AND MASTER

Recreate a Victorian atmosphere of illicit fun and foreplay in your own version of 'upstairs, downstairs.' You and your partner can be master of the house and pretty servant girl for an afternoon break.

The difference between the classes was never so much fun as when master charmed chambermaid and whisked her away to his boudoir for a kinky dusting down.

In Victorian times, sex was taboo in public but much enjoyed in private, as could be seen by the number and popularity of children born to families before the age of birth control.

SEXY ROMP

Since the so-called fragile ladies of the time were supposed to be shy and coy when it came to carnal pleasures, the man of the house would often engage in a sexy romp with his favorite pretty serving girl. But little did he guess that the lady of the house was likely to be doing the same with the most handsome and willing boy she could find.

BRISK FUN

Be sure to dress for your mansion house play – this is half the fun. Why not go turn of the century and dress the master as a stern, Victorian authoritative figure who melts under the influence of the frisky maid's charms. He can wear a black suit with a stuffy shirt and high starched collar. A vest with a crisp handkerchief and watch and chain will complete the look. For a really authentic touch, paint on a large curled moustache often sported by men of the period. You could go to a costume shop and buy a beard to match his hair color for that fetching patriarchal look.

The maid must look pleasantly archaic in a starched black uniform with white apron and hat. Of course, every self-respecting serving wench will want to don sexy underwear, a lacy bra or boned camisole with barely-there panties to please her frolicsome master. She can also wear a garter belt and sexy, sheer stockings with high heels for a modern touch to mix with the Victorian feel of her outfit. Ideally she will wear many

▲ *Recreate the Victorian boudoir in your own home – all you need are some old-fashioned clothes and a few simple props.*

lacy, thin layers which can be peeled off when the play gets intense.

Start off slowly with the maid going about her daily cleaning in the master bedroom, where she is taken by surprise when the master comes in unexpectedly from surveying his fields.

BUXOM BREASTS

She can be coy and blushing at first as he grabs her by the hand and kisses her moist lips. Then she may suddenly become bold and start to unfasten his tie and collar, moving her buxom breasts ever closer to his chest. He will of course be eager to disrobe his favorite servant, and will run his hands searchingly down the front of her uniform, sometimes under her skirt, unfastening buttons and clasps as he goes.

PROPS

As one item of clothing after the next falls to the floor, the master and maid can play with props such as cleaning materials and a laundry basket full of clothes. Perhaps she can dress him in a skirt for fun, or he can place his tie

▲ *The master beckons you into the bedroom and in the build-up to your boudoir romp, you slowly unbutton his vest and shirt.*

around her waist while giving her little pecks on the cheeks, arms and tummy. She can pretend that she spies a stain on the headboard and as she bends over to polish it, he may dust her bare buttocks with a sensuous feather duster.

As she nonchalantly continues her

◄ *As the master tantalizingly peels off your stockings and underwear, you slowly submit to his passionate advances and let him fondle your buttocks and breasts.*

WHY NOT...

• REVERSE ROLES AND LET HER BE THE LADY OF THE HOUSE WHO LONGS FOR SOME INSTRUCTION IN THE EARTHY WAYS OF THE COMMON FOLK. HE CAN PLAY THE GAMEKEEPER WHO IS MORE THAN EAGER TO TEACH HIS LADY AN AMOROUS TRICK OR TWO.

• FOR A WICKED WEEKEND AWAY, THE MASTER CAN KIDNAP THE UNSUSPECTING MAID AND WHISK HER TO A SECRET LOCATION WHERE SHE MUST DO AS HE BIDS.

• MAKE LOVE IN THE MIDDLE OF A FORMAL DINNER TABLE.

▲ *Make mad, passionate love – perhaps in the 'doggy' position at the climax to your master and maidservant romp.*

polishing, he can force her legs slightly apart and tickle the insides while she pretends not to notice.

MASSAGE

The master may then pretend he is tired and simply must lie down on the bed. He exclaims that he would like his shoulders massaged, and his faithful maid sits astride him rubbing them, her breasts bulging tantalizingly close to his face. As he sticks his tongue out to reach her nipples, she teasingly draws away and runs her fingers down his torso. This play can go on endlessly until they

are both as hot as they can stand.

For being such a good maid, the master may then feel that she deserves a special bonus. As he gently nudges her kneeling form up against the bed, she will enjoy his probing leg pushed up longingly between her legs. At the same time, he can cup her breasts in his hands and suck on the back of her neck as he presses his bare chest tenderly against her soft, naked back. Soon he will put his member in fully as they both enjoy the passionate pushing and shoving that completes a happy session of abandoned afternoon lovemaking. ❤

BOSS AND SECRETARY

Do you like your man in his weekday white shirts? Does he look really sexy in a suit? Then why not make the most of his office attire and seduce him in a fantasy power game of 'Boss and Secretary.'

*I*s your fantasy a smouldering vamp of a secretary, oozing sexuality? Or a powerful, sexy boss, who transforms himself into an electrifying lover? Then, why not act out the scene with your partner at home.

LOOK SMART
There is a distinct sexiness in dressing well – he should wear a suit, or just pants, shirt and tie while she should wear stockings and high heels, a fitted skirt and blouse or a figure-hugging suit

◀◀▲ *Act out your power fantasy by dressing seductively as boss and secretary in the privacy of your home. As your boss discusses business, start revealing what else you have in mind...*

◀ *As you talk, the phone rings and you answer it, revealing your stocking tops. Your boss's attention is now caught.*

for her role as the smouldering secretary.

You don't need props to set the scene, just a table and chair. These simple objects can increase the scope of your lovemaking and add excitement to it.

SCENARIO 1

You are in your secretary's office. A document needs typing and you want to explain it to her. She has just gone out to

▶ *While you are distracted on the phone, your boss removes your skirt to reveal another surprise – a g-string!*

▼ *Once your intentions are clear, begin to remove your boss's clothes for the next stage of the business meeting.*

make coffee so you make yourself comfortable in her chair while you read through the papers. When she returns she urges you not to get up, and sits on the corner of the desk, leaning over while you discuss the work.

It is warm in the office, and you find her proximity disconcerting. Her perfume fills the air and, as she leans forward, you find that your eyes are level with her breasts. You try to move away, but suddenly she is behind you, massaging your shoulders.

She loosens your tie, and slides her fingers down between your shirt and your skin. You are being seduced, and there is nothing to do but surrender.

She removes your clothes, and covers your body with kisses, teasing your nipples with her teeth and running her tongue down towards your genitals. She

takes your penis in her mouth, tracing patterns along it with her tongue.

When you are about to orgasm, you find yourself beneath her. She takes your penis inside her, and begins to gyrate, while your body explodes in an orgasm.

SCENARIO 2

Your boss calls you into his office. He is sitting in his leather swivel chair behind a glass-topped desk. It's late but he wants your opinion on some photos for a new advertising campaign on lingerie.

As you proceed through the photos, the shots get more wanton – first the couple are embracing, then they are touching each other in a suggestive manner, then clearly making love.

Embarrassed, you can feel yourself becoming aroused by the pictures. Your hands are beginning to tremble as you turn each new shot.

Your boss leans closer. You are almost finished when suddenly he takes you by the arms and pulls you up beside the chair, kissing you hard on the lips. Before you have recovered your senses, he lifts you on to the glass-topped table and slides his hand up your skirt, lingering on the contrast between your soft skin and the lace of your stocking tops. Then he slowly explores your vulva, making you tremble.

Leaving you motionless on the table he quickly removes all his clothes, then, dressed as you are, he enters you. As you make love, your every move is mirrored in the glass of the table. ❤

▲ *With the phone off the hook, you can get down to business. As your boss is already seated, why not join him?*

◀ *Tables and chairs are excellent props during loveplay. As your boss is on the phone, lay him on the desk and use the woman-on-top position for maximum control. Continue until your boss abandons the meeting.*

▶ *With the boss back in control, the secretary sits back on the desk while he enters her from a standing position.*

TEACHER'S PET

Slip into a fantasy world where you are back at school, fulfil the daydreams of your adolescence in the kinkiest of all role-playing games and give new meaning to being teacher's pet!

Teacher and pupil role-playing games offer endless scope for sexual fun. Once into your chosen character you can wave goodbye to your inhibitions and let your imagination take you to a world where almost anything is permissible. So lock the bedroom door and prepare for some thrilling and unusual extra-curricular activities.

You don't need any props for your game, just a vivid imagination to act out the fantasies in your mind. Here is one schoolboy fantasy – but there are hundreds more out there just waiting for you to make them happen.

DETENTION

The afternoon is hot and everyone else in the school has gone home. You are writing an essay on 'Why I must not talk

▲ *The blackboard is covered in figures but they are not the sort of figures that you have in mind as teacher leans over and you offer her an apple in the hope of winning favor and becoming her pet.*

103

◄ Lesson Number One: never rush a lady when she is undressing! But she may welcome an encouraging caress on her silk-smooth calf.

► Lesson Number Two: When teacher says 'Turn around!' it's best to obey otherwise she may change her mind and call off the lesson.

in class' but you would rather be out playing soccer with your friends. Teacher is busy preparing tomorrow's math lesson on the blackboard when suddenly she drops her chalk. You glance up as she bends down to pick it up and catch an inviting glimpse of a smoothly stockinged thigh under her severe teacher's garb.

You are quite excited – it's almost worth the detention to have seen such a sight. Lucky for you that she didn't see you looking. She busies herself at the blackboard and you try to concentrate on the essay, but it's no longer the thought of your friends playing soccer that's making you lose concentration.

LINES OF COMMUNICATION

Glancing up again you see that she is writing something at the very top of the blackboard and that her skirt has ridden right up the back of her legs. She's wearing stockings! They're held up by the dainty little garter belt that she is wearing on top of lace panties that leave little to the imagination.

You look down at your paper and you are horrified to see what you have written. 'I must not talk in class because it puts others off their work and I would

love to stroke that devastatingly tempting piece of flesh between the top of teacher's stockings and the bottom of her panties.'

Suddenly you hear the sound of chalk rolling across the floor. You look down and see it at your feet. You bend to pick it up and as you look up again you find yourself staring at a pair of the shapliest ankles you have ever seen. You sit up straight to give teacher her chalk back and she looks down at you

▼ Why does teacher want your trousers off? Is she going to beat some sense into you or does she have something else in mind ?

tantalizingly. 'That's not what I asked you to write,' she says. 'Now give me my chalk and get back to work while I decide on a punishment suitable for such naughtiness.'

A STRAPPING LASS

Your imagination races as you wonder what she has in store for you. Perhaps she plans to bend you over the desk and spank you!

She holds her hand out to take the chalk from you and as she does she smiles and says, 'When I was at college, I remember that one of our teachers told us that one way to punish bad behavior was to force bad boys to act out their fantasies in public. But I don't think we need an audience, do we?'

'No, Miss!' you whisper, as you are swept into an erotic world that is certainly not on the curriculum.

So much for the math teacher. Once you've learned what she has to teach you, remember the pretty gym teacher, the frolicsome new French teacher and all the other mistresses in your fantasy sex school. Try out different scenarios and reverse roles.   ♥

▶ *Teacher knows best how to make homework a pure pleasure for this lusty lad. But he may need another lesson or two before he gets it quite right for her.*

▼ *And he is quick to learn that there's more than one way to please teacher.*

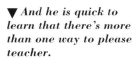

WHY NOT...

TRY TO FIND YOUR OLD SCHOOL CLOTHES, OR SOMETHING SIMILAR – EVEN IF YOU ONLY HAVE AN OLD PAIR OF JEANS OR SWEATER, YOU CAN STILL PUT THEM TO GOOD USE IN A NAUGHTY BEDROOM GAME.

HIRE A GRADUATION GOWN FROM A FANCY DRESS SHOP TO ADD SOME AUTHENTICITY TO YOUR GAMES.

WATCH OLD TV PROGRAMS OR FILMS FEATURING SCHOOLS AND SCHOOL LIFE WHICH MAY GIVE YOU SOME GOOD IDEAS AS TO HOW TO EMBELLISH YOUR FANTASIES.

COURTESANS AND GEISHAS

Offer your partner a taste of the exotic east, and make love to him using the special skills of the revered Japanese courtesans and geishas.

The courtesan and geisha held a unique place in Japanese society. For many centuries, their training and expertise in the ways of love and pleasing men superseded that of their western sisters, and their ethereal charm inspired legends as great as that of the tragic *Madame Butterfly*.

THE GEISHA

The concept of the geisha has no equivalent in other societies. The geisha existed, and still exists, to provide men with all those non-sexual pleasures of the sociable sort, including intellectual stimulation.

As it was deftly put, 'The virgin excites the ardor of your penis, the geisha gives it a little wit and much wisdom.'

In the city of Edo (now Tokyo), the geisha-to-be began learning her craft from the age of ten. She was taught to paint her face with a distinctive white make-up, thus highlighting the vermilion lips and delicate black eyebrows.

ESSENTIAL SKILLS

She was dressed in a gorgeous kimono, and then painstakingly instructed in carriage and movement, the skills of the hostess and the elaborate tea ceremony – indeed everything one would expect from a good finishing school for young ladies.

And it did not end there. The child was taught classical dance and music, so that she would eventually be able to entertain her clients. She received a lit-

▲ *Drive your partner wild with desire by using the seduction skills of a high-class courtesan of ancient Japan. Remember that your sole aim is to please your noble and illustrious client.*

erary education so that she would be able to converse intelligently.

A PRIZED CONFIDANTE

Once launched into the world, the geisha might find herself influential as a negotiator or mediator in political or commercial disputes.

While the young girl continued with her general education, she now embarked on learning the particular skills of her future job.

This on-the-spot training began with careful observation of her friend and tutor at work. She would either peep through cracks in the partition blinds that served as room dividers, or more directly through a half-open door. From such a vantage point, she would be able to take in every detail as her tutor displayed the rich range of her sexual repertoire. In particular she would note the male response to her tutor's expert technique, from arousal to orgasm.

THE PATH TO SUCCESS

By the age of 15, she was considered ready to take up her vocation. She had to find a client whose complete satisfaction with her was demonstrable – shown by his generosity and the frequency of his visits. The quicker he did this the quicker she achieved senior status, which meant a room of her own and perhaps a novice or two whom she in turn would begin to train.

If she was exceptionally gifted at her vocation, she would find herself living in the utmost splendor, pampered by

Her discretion made her privy to confidences, and the workings of the minds of influential men. She might easily marry well. While generally as a geisha she was not exploited sexually, advancing age or some misfortune might cause her to cross the divide into prostitution, the realm of her sister, the courtesan.

▲ ▼ Be as abandoned and as experimental as you like. The ancient Japanese believed that sexual pleasure was the greatest of all and therefore should be indulged in as frequently as possible, as well as in the most exciting manner possible.

THE COURTESAN

Courtesans or 'oirans' as they were called began life with a similar training to the geishas. As children, they learned to sing and dance, and the complex ritual of the tea ceremony.

Then, around the age of 12, they entered a 'green house,' a brothel, under the strict supervision of one of the experienced oirans, who acted as both protector and tutor.

wealthy clients and often able to wield considerable influence, like the powerful mistresses of European tradition.

PLAY THE PART

Elaborate tea ceremonies and polite conversation may be taking things too far in today's society, but there is no reason why you can't borrow some skills from the courtesans and geishas of yesteryear with which to delight your partner.

Begin with a long, solitary scented bath. Choose flowery essential oils – vanilla, ylang ylang or tea rose, and bask in the perfumed water, thinking of the divine form of your partner's body.

Pat yourself dry, apply some perfume and slip on a kimono (or slinky bath robe). Prepare a pot of jasmine tea, put on some soothing music and present him with the mild, scented tea on a tray.

The aim is to please, so you have to use all your powers of seduction to drive your lover wild, while taking your lead from him.

Start by giving him a gentle massage – go for whichever part he likes best and caress him with supple fingers until he becomes aroused.

Let your kimono slip slowly apart, and when he has given you an indica-

▲ *It was not just the courtesans who aimed to please. Japanese lovers in general recognized the importance of oral sex, foreplay and afterplay.*

tion of what he wants you to do, carry out his bidding with passion and fervor, bringing him to new heights of sexual pleasure.

REVEALING YOUR SKILLS

Imagine you are a high-class courtesan and he your powerful client, and your aim is to give as much pleasure as is humanly possible within the walls of your perfumed boudoir.

You might even have a novice, who you are tutoring in the ways of love, watching you from a crack in the door, and it is your duty to reveal to her all the tricks and the skills you have learned in the course of your sexual training.

When your repertoire has been exhausted, and your partner too, you may want to persuade him that playing the courtesan is fun, and that there is no reason why he shouldn't take on the role and please you next time you make love. ♥

TIPS FOR LOVERS

THE ANCIENT JAPANESE WERE SERIOUS ABOUT SEXUAL PLEASURE AND DIRECT WHEN GIVING ADVICE:

'IF YOU PLANT YOUR KNIFE IN A TUFT OF SPRING GRASS, PUSH IT IN AS FAR AS THE ROOT.'

SOMETIMES THE ADVICE WOULD BE COUCHED IN METAPHOR AS THIS DESCRIPTION OF REAR ENTRY SHOWS:

'WHILE AWAITING THE SEED, THE WOMAN IS LIKE THE EARTH, SHE LIKES TO BE TURNED OVER.'

YET THE TECHNIQUES WERE NOT ENTIRELY DEVOID OF EMOTION AND CONSIDERATION. AS WELL AS RECOGNIZING THE VALUE OF AFTERPLAY, IT WAS UNDERSTOOD THAT THE POLITE LOVER WOULD NOT DENY HIS PARTNER THE PLEASURE OF POST-COITAL BLISS:

'ON BOARD THE FLOATING WORLD OF PLEASURES, THE GOOD SAILOR DOES NOT DREAM OF GOING ASHORE AGAIN.'

THE HAPPY HOOKER

Viva vice! It may be a deadly sin, but it can make for memorable sex, especially if you dress and undress to play the happy hooker to a partner on the lookout for an unforgettable night of lust.

▲ *If you are going to spring a surprise on your partner out of doors, remember to do it somewhere out of sight of the neighbors. What's on offer is definitely for his eyes only.*

No one knows why some men find prostitutes so exciting. There are, of course, unattached men for whom hookers are the only sexual partners. But there are many married men who are happy to pay for sex – perhaps because they want to spice up their sex lives in ways they don't want their partners to know about. Most prosti-tutes are in it for the money, but there are many who enjoy the element of danger their work gives them, and some who are as erotically enthusiastic as their clients.

SURPRISE! SURPRISE!

Playing the happy hooker to a lad with lusty loins allows you both to turn a run-

WHY NOT...

HAM UP YOUR HAPPY HOOKER ROMPS
WITH SCENES FROM FILMS THAT
FEATURED CELEBRATED PROSTITUTES/
VAMPS/TEMPTRESSES. FOR
INSPIRATION, AND COLORFUL IDEAS ON
COSTUMES, WATCH:
• *IRMA LA DOUCE*, A MUSICAL BY
BILLY WILDER, ABOUT A PARIS
POLICEMAN WHO FALLS FOR A
PROSTITUTE AND BECOMES HER PIMP.
• *THE BLUE ANGEL*, STARRING
MARLENE DIETRICH AS A NIGHTCLUB
SINGER/TEMPTRESS.
• *CABARET*, FEATURING LIZA MINNELLI
AS A SEXY SINGER AND DANCER IN THE
DECADENT THIRTIES IN BERLIN.

of-the-mill session into a steamy scenario for sensational sex.

Imagine his surprise when he turns the car into the drive and sees a sexy siren step out of the shadows, giving him a tantalizing glimpse of cleavage as she bends over to breathe huskily, 'Hey there! Want some action?'

Or maybe he comes home to find the bedroom has been transformed into a bordello, the unmistakable aroma of lust in the air ... and a partner with the promise of a night to remember pouting her pretty lips.

WHAT'S THE COST?

No matter where he is importuned by his partner – in the drive, in the bedroom, even in a pre-arranged spot – the first thing he notices is that she is wearing very little under her coat: a glimpse of bare breast and a flash of aroused nipple sees to that.

She may tantalize him by kissing him full on the mouth and, when he responds, drawing away mockingly. Or perhaps she lets her solicitous fingers

▲ *Look the part: wear something very special. And change the lighting to add a warm glow to the business in hand.*

▼ *Being on top of the situation is all part of the prostitute's job. If that's what he wants, dig your heels in.*

brush against his crotch and leaves them there for a moment or two so that he knows that sex is definitely on the menu – at a price.

WHAT'S ON OFFER?

Lowering her voice to a seductive husk she tells him what's on offer, letting her tongue flick around his ear as she whispers the various ways she can pleasure

Maybe it's a black bra, black stockings or fishnets and a garter belt made of soft, yielding leather – just the thing to whip him up into a frenzy. And if he is turned on by a light lash of leather, well, he who pays the piper...

Or maybe he enjoys some spanking good fun. Or if he likes the innocent, virginal type, wear a white, lacy bra, a snowy-white garter belt with a gleaming pair of spilt-crotch panties, all the sexier if they are fringed with soft swansdown.

THE MAGIC MOMENT

Let his fantasies take flight! The more aroused he becomes, the sexier you will feel, too, until that magic moment when you both know you can't bear it much longer and you are as desperate to yield your loins to him as he is to enter you. But do your best to bear the voluptuous volcano erupting into your every nerve ending for just a few more fantasy-filled moments until you climax together in a simultaneous explosion of ecstasy.

And now? It's his turn to do the work, and her turn to let him do it. ❤

him and for how much.

'You want it straight? That's going to cost you a drink or two.

'Fellatio? It takes two to tango.'

'A little hanky-spanky. I love a man who can take it lying down! And give it too! Know what I mean?'

And all the time she's talking, her hands and lips are playing with what she knows from experience are his most sensitive places.

UNDRESSED TO THRILL

Keeping her coat on, she unknots his tie and lazily pulls it from under his collar, making it plain that there's something else she'd rather be pulling!

Still in her coat, she unbuttons his shirt, one button at a time, licking his chest as she bares it.

Kneeling down, she takes his shoes and socks off, massages his feet and then gradually lets her hands run up and down his calves and thighs.

She helps him out of his trousers and, seeing his desire rising in front of her, she stands up, lazily shrugs her shoulders and lets her coat slowly fall to the ground, revealing the special outfit that she knows is going to bring him to a peak of passion.

▲ *Girls who take their business seriously often find that being astride things maximizes the client's penetration.*

▼ *Some prostitutes bend over backwards to please their clients. Others find that bending over forwards is equally satisfying!*

ROMAN ROMP

Take yourselves on a trip back in time to the most sensual and decadent of all civilizations and partake in the extraordinary physical pleasures of ancient Rome.

▲ *As a tasty prelude to your Roman romp, feed each other tidbits from the delicacies of the table as you sip chilled wine from glass goblets.*

Like many famous legends of the past, the great orgies of ancient Rome are little more than a myth. There is no doubt that some citizens enjoyed the pleasures of the flesh in great numbers, but the ordinary man and woman's sexual activities were of a more modest and ordinary kind.

Nevertheless, the Romans possessed a rich sensuality and an appreciation of physical pleasure which has almost been lost to the modern world. The warm climate, an abundance of fresh and delicious food and plenty of leisure ensured that there was both the time and inclination for love.

With a few props and very little planning, you can create the atmosphere of ancient Rome in your own home, and submit to an orgy of pleasure for a day.

THE ROMAN BATHS

One of the greatest of all legacies bestowed by the Romans is the bath. In the ancient world the bath was not just considered as a simple means of getting clean, it was a form of recreation, a way of relaxing and socializing. The humblest citizens could enjoy the pleasures of the huge and cavernous public baths, while the nobility had their very own bathing halls in which to while away the mornings and afternoons.

Your modern bathroom may be a more humble affair, but it is the perfect place to begin your orgy of pleasure. Run a warm bath, and sprinkle it liberally with scented oil. Take it in turns to soak in the perfumed water, or if the tub is big enough, you can bathe together. Make it a really sensual experience, using large sponges soaked alternately in buckets of hot and cold water to shower each other's skin. Choose natural, traditionally scented soaps and shampoos, with perfume such as lemon verbena or lavender, and above all take your time, sensuously washing every inch of your partner's body.

Clean and refreshed, next on the agenda is a Roman body massage with

neath! Dress as if preparing to attend a banquet, and don't restrict yourselves to white sheets or muslin – the Romans favored brilliant jewel colors such as saffron and flame red, purple and gold. Use colored scarves and jewelry to enhance your toga, and the woman can prepare her hair in a beautifully elaborate, exotic style.

A FEAST OF PLEASURE

Once dressed, you are now ready for the great feast. Romans ate their meals while reclining on couches. This was considered a sign of refinement and social position (only slaves sat at the table, receiving permission to recline only on public holidays). Return to the massage cushions on the floor or recline on a low sofa, and place the trays of food on a coffee table or the floor.

Put rolls, cheese, cold meat, small sausages, paté on toast, or anything for that matter that you enjoy. Make sure there is plenty of fresh fruit – peaches, pineapples, pomegranates, passion fruit, figs and, of course, lush, juicy grapes. Serve everything with copious quantities of chilled wine, which you should

rich oils. Lay cushions on the floor and cover them with fresh towels, then take it in turns to cover each other's body with the scented oil. Make it an invigorating, firm massage, otherwise the relaxation may send either one of you to sleep! Once the whole body is glistening, take a small, blunt scraper (a credit card will do) and gently scrape all the oil off the body in soft movements in the direction of the heart. You can wipe the excess oil on a paper towel. This exfoliation should leave the skin tingling and feeling super-smooth.

▲ ▼ You might like to work up an appetite first with some quickie sex, then lounge around in post-coital bliss.

ROMAN DRESS

Now you are ready to put on your Roman clothes. Tunics covered by simply draped lengths of fabric are among the easiest of costumes to emulate. You can surprise one another by preparing your costumes in private. Make them as sexy as you dare and, of course, you don't need to wear anything under-

ROMAN ROLES

THOSE INTO ROLE-PLAY CAN GO WILD WITH THE ROMAN THEME. YOU CAN PLAY MASTER AND MISTRESS OF THE EMPIRE, FEASTING AND COPULATING UNTIL DAWN, OR MASTER/MISTRESS AND SLAVE, THE SLAVE READY AT ALL TIMES TO FULFIL EVERY SEXUAL WHIM. PLAY ROMAN CENTURION AND VESTAL VIRGIN, OR GLADIATOR AND NOBLE LADY. ONE CAN RAVISH OR SEDUCE THE OTHER, THE MEN HAVING RETURNED FROM BATTLE, AND THE WOMEN HAVING ESCAPED THE RESTRICTING CHAINS OF THEIR PROTECTORS FOR A NIGHT OF PASSION.

▶ *Aim for simultaneous orgasm as the grand finale to your orgy. If you don't achieve it, you will at least have had fun!*

drink from goblet-shaped glasses.

Play games if you feel like it – eat food from one another's body, try passing the wine from one mouth to another without spilling a drop, or try catching grapes in your mouths – if they fall, you have to perform a forfeit.

TUG OF LOVE

Revived by the food and wine, you can enjoy each other's body again. This time you can undress each other completely if you choose – a simple tug should free each of you from the restrictions of your robes. Comfortable on a bed of cushions, you can experiment with athletic positions, or, satiated with food and sex, resort to the easiest and most gratifying. Whatever you get up to, make it a night to remember! ❤

GYM INSTRUCTOR

A workout with your partner can lead to a whole lot more than just well-toned muscles – you may end up exercising your lovemaking skills too!

Regular exercise is good for your sex life. It improves your stamina, flexibility and muscle tone, and gives you the strength and agility to make love in many of the more physically complex positions.

Whether you belong to a gym or exercise at home, the benefits are enormous. However, when working out at home, it is best to go it alone if you are really serious about fitness.

Of course you can exercise with your partner – but beware. The proximity of your near-naked bodies, the pink, flushed cheeks following exertion and the faint odor of clean sweat often adds up to a positive invitation to intercourse! So, if you do decide to work out together, be prepared for your thoughts to turn from your intended task.

TWO'S COMPANY

Whatever happens on the gym mat, working out together can be tremendous fun, and extremely stimulating – you can help each other with the trickier exercises, all the while appreciating the unique beauty of your partner's body.

Choose a time when you won't be disturbed for an hour or so, and change into comfortable clothes.

Put on some music with a good beat if it helps, and start with some simple warming-up exercises. Straightforward stretching or jogging on the spot will do. Then follow your usual routine, adding some simple movements where you have contact with your partner.

Sit-ups are often the most difficult to

achieve alone, because you need something solid on which to anchor your feet. Have your partner sit at your feet and hold your ankles while you perform as many sit-ups as you are reasonably able.

By now, if you are reasonably fit, you should feel aglow with life and

▲ *Your partner may display all the signs of a tough trainer who wants to put you through your paces – but with a little persuasion he could have a surprising change of heart.*

energy, and more than prepared for whatever happens next.

FANTASY WORKOUT

If your fantasies include images of muscle-bound men and 'personal trainers' or lithe, fit aerobics instructors in shiny lycra, now is your chance to play out those erotic dreams with your partner.

Let your imagination transport you to a faraway gymnasium, deserted but for yourselves. The faint odor of rubber exercise mats, the old wood and suede of the gymnasium horse and the polished, sprung wooden floor will take you back to your school days. But now you are an adult with adult desires to match!

As you watch him vault the horse several times with ease, you marvel at his strength and lust after the fine form of his muscular body.

Your desire inflames: as he performs

▶ *Flexing those muscles together can have you both working up a sweat for a very different reason!*

▼ *If your partner is hot from all the hard work, you can soon make him even hotter by initiating a bout of athletic foreplay.*

DOS AND DON'TS

• DO WARM UP PROPERLY FIRST. OTHERWISE YOU RISK PAINFUL PULLED MUSCLES IF YOUR MOVEMENTS ARE TOO VIGOROUS TO BEGIN WITH.

• DO MAKE SURE YOU HAVE ENOUGH SPACE. A BADLY AIMED LEG-SWING CAN CAUSE A CONSIDERABLE AMOUNT OF DAMAGE TO YOUR SURROUNDINGS AND YOUR PARTNER.

• DON'T GET CARRIED AWAY AND EXERCISE TOO MUCH. YOU WILL BE TOO TIRED FOR LOVEMAKING AND YOUR MUSCLES WILL BE STIFF THE FOLLOWING DAY.

◀ *You don't have to abandon your exercise routine completely. You can incorporate some of your movements into your lovemaking. But you will probably find that some of your clothes just have to go.*

▼ *If your gymnastic workout is for real, don't stick to a rigid routine if you would rather make love. If, of course, you've simply been acting out a fantasy, then there is no limit to how far you can push your body, driving each other wild with desire in the process!*

push-ups on the gymnasium mat, you imagine you are lying naked beneath him and he is teasing your taut, waiting body with his penis, the form of which is just visible through his exercise shorts.

Now it is your turn to vault the horse. You leap and clear the horse with ease, but he is waiting to catch you. With a swift movement, he removes your T-shirt and shorts and lifts you back on to the horse, caressing every inch of your perspiring body with firm hands.

His arms are so strong, you feel like a mere plaything in his hands, yet his fingers find your clitoris with ease and he brings you to a sensational climax.

Before you have recovered your senses, he spins you round to face the soft suede body of the horse and enters you, firmly but gently, holding your hips and teasing the soft skin of your back with his tongue. You reach orgasm simultaneously, and your fantasy dissolves in a rainbow of light and pleasure. ❤

4

Seductive Situations

It is very easy to restrict your lovemaking solely to the bedroom, or to squeeze it in between family and work commitments. Instead, you should set aside time and make an effort to entice each other into the mood for romance. With a little bit of planning and a desire to seduce, there are many every-day events, whether a telephone call or an evening meal, which can be turned into a sexy occasion. Use your surroundings to further your excitement in each other and achieve previously unknown feelings of pleasure.

A TIME FOR TWO

Putting time aside to really enjoy lovemaking can sometimes be very difficult to organize, but isn't it worth it? Forget the worries of the day; a little pampering goes a long way.

▲ *Tonight there is no need to undress quickly, you can both take it slowly. What's the rush? After all, you have all night to play.*

Considering the huge stresses and pressures of daily life it is no surprise that sex with your partner can often become a little routine: after a busy day at work and looking after children, time for just the two of you is often neglected. You can't afford to let this happen. Every relationship needs a little pepping up. So why not give your sex life a boost by treating yourselves to a night neither of you will forget?

To guarantee a truly memorable night, you have to start preparing during the day. Wake up a little earlier than usual and spend time kissing, cuddling and simply turning each other on. You won't have time to make love, but that's the point – you are teasing each other, building up the anticipation of what the night ahead has in store. By the time you both leave for work, you'll be aching to see each other that evening.

Do anything that will make you look and feel thoroughly gorgeous and desirable – go the the gym and work out; have a facial; wax your legs; have your hair done. To truly get you in the mood, why not go to a sexy movie on your own? There's nothing as decadent and horny as watching a sexy film during the day. You might even get some ideas for the evening.

So you're physically and mentally ready but you also need an environment that is conducive to wonderful lovemaking. Make your home perfect for the ideal evening before you go out. That way, when you return, your home enhances your mood, not snaps you out of it.

PREPARE YOUR HOME

If you have children, pack them off to a friend or relative for the entire night. If you share an apartment make sure your roommates are out of the way – you don't want them disturbing you tonight. Stock your fridge with some champagne and your favorite foods:

Tease your partner a little, ring him or her up and tell them to wait by the fax machine for a top-secret thrill. Send him or her a provocative message outlining your sexy intentions. A day at the office will never seem such fun, or pass so slowly!

PAMPER YOURSELF

Mentally preparing yourself isn't enough to guarantee an evening in sex heaven – you need to feel fantastic physically too. So pamper yourself. If you're at home, you have all day to prepare, but if you're working, try to leave an hour early. You can always catch up with your work and, let's face it, in the morning you won't care if your boss complains.

▲ *Less rush – more fuss. It's much more tormenting to slowly undress your partner, and look at each other's bodies as if for the very first time.*

▶ *A delicious, slow, sensuous massage is a perfect prelude to wonderful sex. Also it really shows your partner what they're missing.*

◄ Tantalize your partner, be imaginative and adventurous. Use all sorts of suggestive toys and sexual aids to extend your foreplay. Experimenting is fun.

▼ By the time you give in to the delights of sex after so much teasing you'll be incredibly turned on and on your way to a mind-blowing experience.

in – this evening your underwear will be on show. Half the thrill of any gift is in the unwrapping.

EAT OUT

Eating at home can be romantic but for a special treat, book a table at your favorite restaurant. Arrive separately so it feels like a date; flirt with each other; play footsie under the table; enjoy each other's company; feed each other suggestively. Try not to talk about work or children or any stressful subjects – this is quality time for the two of you to get to know each other again, to remind yourselves of why you love each other. Have a leisurely meal but don't drink or eat too much. You don't want to get home feeling drunk, fat and bloated, too lethargic for lovemaking.

strawberries, chocolates, ice-cream and crudités can all stave off après-sex munchies. They can also be used to great effect during sex itself. Let your imagination go wild!

Take the phone off the hook – now is not the best time for your mother to ring – and turn your bedroom into a sex haven. You could dim the lights; arrange some candles around the room; select some sensual music; put crisp, clean sheets on the bed and turn the heating up.

Make sure any sex accessories you might use (erotic books, sex toys, oils, condoms and tissues) are easily at hand. Your bedroom is now the perfect magical setting for you and your partner to be intimate and completely uninhibited.

Everything is ready now; all you have to do is get dressed. Leggings and T-shirts may be your normal attire, but for this to be special, you need to feel special. Wear an outfit that you feel sensational in – one that you know your partner loves you in or maybe something you've bought especially for tonight. Wear underwear that you feel sexy and seductive

After dinner, catch a cab home and smooch in the back seat. Cab rides can be incredible turn-ons. You can fumble and fondle but don't forget, there is only so far you can go without upsetting the driver. When you get home you'll be pleased you prepared the place beforehand. Coming home to a sinkful of dishes and the children screaming at each other would destroy all the good work you've done.

INDULGE EACH OTHER

Home alone, you can really enjoy each other. Take a candelit bath together and spend ages soaping and caressing your bodies. When you are ready, towel each other dry. Take a bottle of champagne into the bedroom, pour a glass each, put some

▶ *A carefully arranged love nest equipped with your favorite food, drink and music can work wonders for dynamic lovemaking.*

music on, light the candles and lie down together. But don't start making love yet. Indulge in a relaxing, sensuous oil massage. Undressing together and then stroking each other lovingly is the perfect prelude to sex.

When you do start to make love, aim to make it last for hours. Tonight isn't about quickie sex – it's about hours spent together, enjoying and relishing each other. Rediscover each other's body; caress each other; talk dirty; share fantasies; watch erotic videos; say what turns you on most about your partner and then start to touch each other sexually. Take it in turns to arouse each other but don't have intercouse until you really can't wait any more.

After a whole day's preparation, the teasing and tantalizing, phone calls and faxes – the anticipation of making love will be incredible for both of you. The sex should live up to your expectations. Enjoy every moment of this special, private time. You both deserve to be fulfilled.   ❤

A NIGHT TO REMEMBER

Spontaneous, spur-of-the-moment sex can be very exciting, but an evening of prolonged and leisurely loveplay is equally fulfilling. So draw the curtains and get ready!

Long and lingering foreplay is the key to a memorable night of passion and for many couples can often take over from actual intercourse as the main source of excitement. But foreplay does not begin at the bedroom door. Sharing a meal and a bottle of wine is a natural prelude to sex, especially when it involves food that recalls an amorous holiday or sexual encounter.

Eating food in a particularly erotic way can act as a remote-control signal to turn your partner on. Spicy food heats the blood, and well-known aphrodisiacs such as oysters and asparagus push up the pulse rate and put many couples in the mood for love.

Dancing is another essential ingredient for sexual arousal, whether it be in the form of a slow, sexy smooch or gyrating to a pulsating beat. And, of course, in the comfort of your own home, there is no need to keep your clothes on!

SEX A-PEEL

Slowly peeling off your partner's clothes, or your own while he or she watches, adds an exciting element to your night of passion. Striptease is one of the most erotic ways of arousing your partner. It is an art well worth perfecting. There's more to it than simply slipping sexily out of what you are wearing. Make sure that you have on several layers of clothes, each one sexier than the one above, and as you strip, dance to music appropriate to the mood you are trying to create: Ravel's *Bolero* is a favorite.

▲ *Feeding each other like this can be the precursor to fantastic foreplay, but don't drink too much. A glass or two can make you shed your inhibitions, but any more than that may make you drowsy. And you don't want to fall asleep for a long, long time.*

Remember, practice makes perfect, so rehearse in front of a full-length mirror to make sure you are making the most of your talent to arouse in this way.

TOUCHING TIMES

In foreplay, touch is all-important. But remember, touch can involve much more than your fingertips. Many people enjoy the warm, stimulating and sensual effects of fur, and feathers can be extremely erotic. Feathers can be used

but stimulating technique to explore different parts of the body.

GIVE IT SOME LIP

The lips can be particularly effective in bringing your partner to the height of sexual arousal. Remember that kissing does not have to be restricted to the mouth. Kissing the throat, the neck, the shoulders, the toes, the soles of the feet, the fingers, the insides of the elbows, the backs of the knees and the genitals, all have their own special sensations. Don't forget the navel and the nipples, and remember that most men's nipples are as sensitive to being caressed by the lips as their partner's. And a light carpet of kisses and caresses laid down and across the whole body can be especially rewarding both for the giver and the person receiving.

to stimulate the nipples and the palms of the hands, on the soles of the feet and on the surface of the skin, rather than used directly on the genitals.

Anticipation is one of the most powerful sex stimulants of all – the idea that you are going to become sexually aroused is exciting in itself. What the French call *pattes d'araignée* – literally spider's feet – takes advantage of this fact. This light, almost tickling massage requires only the lightest touch of the tips of the fingers.

The aim is not actually to touch the skin – merely the tips of the hairs that grow on it. Try giving your partner a spider massage in sensitive areas such as the nipples, the chest, the scrotum, the area around the anus and the insides of the thighs.

The anticipation factor is increased if the hands seem to be moving slowly and enticingly towards the genitals. Your partner will be hankering for the final touch – but it never comes. Just as he or she is getting used to the sweep of one hand, the other can take over in a new and unexpected area. Use this subtle

▲▼ *A well-practiced striptease can arouse a partner to such a point that he or she is powerless to do anything other that join in and turn a sexy solo into a delightful duet.*

KEEP IT COOL

Water and ice can also have a stimulating shock effect on the skin. Use ice which is on the point of melting to leave deliciously cool, damp trails across the entire length of the body. A single touch

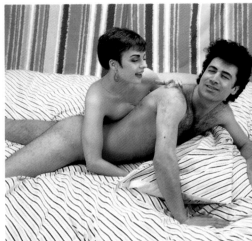

with an ice cube on a nipple will have it erect in seconds, and many find the cold kiss of ice on the genitals a turn-on during the build-up to intercourse.

Ice can also be used to wonderful effect when foreplay gives way to intercourse. If at the moment of climax, with the woman on top, squatting over her partner and with his penis inside her, she rubs ice cubes into his groin, he will be unable to stop himself thrusting deeper and deeper into her as he ejaculates, making it a memorable climax.

A Gentle Blow

Blowing on wet skin produces goose pimples and the resulting tightening of the skin can be a major turn-on. The best way is to moisten the skin with the tongue and blow across the wet area. Remember that your breath on your partner's face – a secondary effect of kissing – can be a sensational experience in itself.

Turkish Delight

Why not indulge in Turkish-type foreplay? Snuggle at the foot of the bed and slowly work your way up, under the covers, using your lips, hands and tongue to arouse your partner as you go. It's one of

▲ ▶ A spider massage or an exhilarating caress on the genitals with an ice cube is all part of the fun of a night indoors.

▼ The soft kiss of a feather floating on the skin arouses, excites and stimulates.

the methods that harem girls used to please their masters, but in these days of sexual equality, there's no reason why the girl shouldn't lie back and enjoy her partner's joyful journey up her body.

A Breath of Warm Air

If you attach some soft feathers to the nozzle of your hairdryer, turn it on and run it all over your partner, you will quickly reduce him or her to a state of such glorious delirium that they will find it difficult to stop themselves exploding in an ecstasy of eroticism. ❤

DINNER FOR TWO

A romantic dinner for two often leads to lovemaking. But if you really want to tickle your partner's sexual taste buds, add a bit of spice to the meal with some French dressing.

Everyone enjoys the luxury of having a special meal cooked for them, and there are few things more appealing than a romantic meal in the privacy of your own home. If dinner for two is a common occurrence in your home, you can make it dinner with a difference and surprise your partner by serving the meal in a special, sexy costume, which should whet their appetite for whatever delights are to come.

SIMPLE PLANNING

There are really only three things to plan – the time of your meal, the menu and the outfit you will be wearing. Choose an evening when you know you won't be disturbed. Try to make sure neighbors don't drop round unexpectedly, and, if you have children, arrange for them to spend the night with friends.

Then think about your menu. A casserole, curry or a similar 'one-pot' meal may not appear to be the sexiest food around, but such dishes are easy to prepare and will keep for hours in the oven if you happen to get distracted before the main course is served.

COSTUME DRAMA

The outfit you choose will make or break the evening, and for most men, the obvious always wins over the subtle. A short skirt and garter belt, with a tight sweater or low-cut blouse is bound to raise his temperature, particularly if he rarely sees you dressed in such a manner. Or you could try a silky kimono-style robe, belted loosely to reveal a lacy

▲ *Set the scene for a romantic meal, and put on a sexy French maid's outfit to really excite and arouse your man. Good wine will enhance your mood for love and by this time he will have no doubt of your intentions.*

leotard and lace-topped stockings beneath.

As you are cooking the meal and playing waitress as well, a French maid's outfit will amuse and tantalize even the most reluctant of men. A short black dress, tiny white apron and bonnet, black stockings and garter belt, and high-heeled shoes – the elements are all fairly straightforward so there is no need to go to the trouble of renting a costume, when

you can probably put it together yourself from your own wardrobe – improvise if necessary.

Don't forget that it's the personal touches which will really thrill him – perhaps you could neglect to wear any panties with your garter belt, or maybe you could wear a black Wonderbra under your outfit – it will make all the difference to your figure.

If the man is cooking and serving the meal, there are all sorts of things which will turn the woman on. Those who can dress Chippendale-style – and get away with it – should do so. Tarzan-style loincloths, sexy strings, or even the bare necessities such as a bow tie and apron should whet her appetite.

Those men who prefer to wear a little more – and have a dinner jacket – could make it a grand 'black tie' event. Their partners can put on all their finery too. Alternatively, make it a 'theme' dinner and dress the part.

GETTING READY

On the evening of the meal, once the main course is cooking in the oven, you

▲ *The soup may be going cold but the mood is really heating up as you administer to his every whim and fantasy.*

▼ *Use table or chairs for convenient support as your passion boils over and you make love over the dining table.*

can prepare the first course. Again make it something simple like shrimp cocktail or a chilled soup which won't spoil if not eaten immediately.

Lay the table in true restaurant style to make the occasion special, and fill small dishes with peanuts and potato chips for your partner to munch with an aperitif – after all, you don't want your lover so hungry that they only have eyes for your chicken casserole.

Place a bottle of their favorite pre-dinner drink next to the potato chips and peanuts, and then retire to get changed into your costume – you may have to get changed in the kitchen if you don't want to spoil the surprise, or perhaps blindfold your 'guest' while he or she munches on the peanuts in order to make your appearance with the first course all the more exciting.

DINNER IS SERVED

When you finally make your entrance, all thoughts of food should fly out of your partner's mind. Brush seductively against his or her body as you place the plates down on the table, leaning down low to adjust the cutlery or bring the salt and pepper closer.

He can caress her all over, performing cunnilingus while stroking her thighs close to her stocking tops and her breasts through her special outfit. Take your time. Everything is planned so that the dinner won't spoil.

MAIN COURSE

When each of you has climaxed, there's no need to stop. Consider your first orgasm as the 'hors d'oeuvre.' Then once you have recovered your energy, you can move on to the 'main course.'

Before he achieves erection again, she can swing around on the dining chair to sit astride him, moving her body rhythmically against his until he becomes hard once more with desire.

JUST DESSERTS

As soon as she feels his penis pressing against her she can take him inside her, gyrating her hips to bring each of them to orgasm for a second time.

Or he can penetrate her from behind, while she uses the dining table or chair as a support, entering her gently while stroking her body with his fingertips.

Then, when you are finally satiated and have untangled yourselves from each other's arms, sup a glass of celebratory wine and start to eat the delicious meal that is waiting for you. ❤

If you can see that they feel obliged to start eating the food you have lovingly prepared straight away, it may take more seductive tactics to lure them away from the green salad.

Unfurl his napkin and place it on his lap, smoothing it out around his thighs and over his trouser fly. Or tie her napkin around her neck, adjusting it over her breasts while softly kissing her hairline. It shouldn't take too much of this special treatment before your partner falls into your arms hungry for love.

▲ Enter your lover from the rear as she leans over the table – the deep penetration is an erotic bonus for both partners.

SPECIALITIES

Now you can serve up the other specialities of the evening. On the dining chair, on the floor, or even on the table, she can take his member in her mouth, closing her lips around it to make pink lipstick rings on the shaft. She can toy with him with her teeth, first sucking the tip of the penis, then running her teeth gently down the shaft to send electric shivers up his spine.

WHY NOT...

• SET THE TABLE IN A SUGGESTIVE FASHION, PLACING THE CUTLERY, CROCKERY, NAPKINS AND TABLE DECORATIONS TO CREATE AMUSING SEXUAL FORMS.

• FLOAT LITTLE BITS OF 'PENIS PASTA' IN YOUR SOUP. THIS KINKY SHAPED PASTA MADE IN THE SHAPE OF A PENIS AND TWO TESTICLES IS AVAILABLE FROM SPECIALIST PASTA SHOPS IN MOST BIG TOWNS AND CITIES.

• MELT AFTER-DINNER MINTS ALL OVER YOUR PARTNER'S BODY AFTER THE MEAL THEN, EVER SO SLOWLY, LICK THEM OFF!

*F*IRESIDE FROLICS

Cold wintry nights are made for love. So lay your lover down beside the light of an open fire and let the burning heat of your passion match the heat of the flames within!

*M*aking love beside an open fire is a rare and special treat. Whether you have a real chimney in your own home, or can only enjoy the pleasure once in a while in the room of a holiday cottage, it is worth taking time and trouble over the planning. A roaring fire will allow you to create the mood for love almost instantly.

Fireside sex adds a primitive dimension to lovemaking, evoking memories of sex from the dawn of time when lovers could give full reign to their passion.

▲▶ *What could be a more perfect end to a special evening than making love in front of a roaring fire? But do ensure that there are enough coals or logs to last while you kiss and slowly undress each other.*

fireplace. Pour yourselves a special drink to get you in the mood – make it something you rarely have, like a rich liqueur or Schnapps, to warm you on the inside while the fire heats you without. If you prefer champagne or sparkling wine, prepare an ice bucket – you can always use the ice as a thrilling aid to foreplay when you start to make love.

Draw all the curtains or blinds and stop any drafts at floor level that may take the heat out of the moment. Stuff towels against the bottom of doors if the winter wind is blowing through, and have extra blankets at hand to wrap yourselves in just in case you cool off in the afterglow.

Turn off all the lights – if you find the light of the flames too dim you can light candles all around the room. Then fetch plenty of wood and stoke up the fire so that it will burn for as long as possible.

HOT LOVE

When you are ready, lie down in front of the fire and undress your partner very slowly. Make the undressing itself a

Such lovemaking should always be something more than just a quickie. After a long country walk, a romp in the snow or a special evening together, making love beside a warm fire can complete a perfect day.

WARMTH AND COMFORT

Once the fire is glowing and the evening is yours, the first thing you should do is to make yourselves really comfortable.

Lay pillows or cushions on the floor, or better still, spread a thick sheepskin rug or feather comforter in front of the

highly erotic part of the foreplay. Remove each article of clothing carefully, kissing and caressing arms, shoulders, neck, breasts, chest and thighs as each new erogenous zone is revealed. Then lay your partner back on the comforter or pillows and caress them gently while they grow accustomed to the natural heat of the flames. Now let your naked partner undress you.

You can kiss, but don't get carried away too soon. Let your bodies bathe in the heat, and watch the firelight flicker and play on each other's skin.

Caressing the mounds and hollows with the tips of your fingers, slide down to kiss your partner's genitals. Take them in your mouth and suck, lick and tease to the point of orgasm. Don't hurry your partner – make the pleasure last as long as possible. Then it's your turn to enjoy the same warming treat.

ALL THE WAY

When the pleasure of oral sex has been given and received, you can lie satisfied in each other's arms, with no sound but one another's heartbeats and the crackle of the flames.

Try not to drift off to sleep. Instead, coax your lover back to arousal and make passionate love again. ♥

▼ Start off in the missionary position and as the flames of passion blaze into an explosion of desire, roll over and over on top of each other, and enjoy the myriad sensations that each change of position brings before melting together in an inferno of passion.

WHY NOT...

TAKE ADVANTAGE OF THE WIDE EXPANSE OF FLOOR SPACE. MOST PEOPLE'S BEDS ARE NOT REALLY BIG ENOUGH TO ALLOW UNRESTRICTED MOVEMENT, SO THIS IS THE TIME TO EXPERIMENT WITH MORE ENERGETIC POSITIONS. FOR EXAMPLE, THE WOMAN CAN SIT ASTRIDE THE SHAFT OF HER PARTNER'S PENIS, THEN SPIN ROUND TO FACE AWAY FROM HIM WITHOUT A CHANGE OF RHYTHM. A DEFT MOVEMENT OF THE LEGS AND HE CAN BE BEHIND HER, MAKING LOVE WITH HER ON ALL FOURS.

SEX OVER THE PHONE

For couples in love separation is the ultimate nightmare, but don't despair – relief is at the other end of the phone. Keep the passion burning and the wires sizzling with lust on the line.

You and your partner may be apart but you can still turn each other on. How? By setting the wires alight with your passion and making love over the phone.

Mention sex over the phone to most people and they automatically think of heavy breathers or 'naughty nympho' sex lines. But there is another type of sexual interaction which is altogether a lot more fun.

If your days at work or home are constantly interrupted by sexy thoughts of your partner and what

▲ *Get yourself in the mood first, then give your lover a surprise that will brighten up his day no end – phone him at work.*

you'd like to be doing with him – or you have to be apart for some reason – you can let him know just how much you miss him by picking up the phone and dialing his number – that's what phones are for!

OFFICE PERKS

If you're at home while your partner is slaving away at work, why not give him a real surprise? To get yourself in the mood before you phone, try remembering a particularly exciting lovemaking session. Re-run it in your mind, recalling every last detail: what you were both wearing; the smell of his aftershave; what you said; what you did to each other and how turned on you felt.

Or you could read your favorite erotic story – if you don't have one, *My Secret Garden* by Nancy Friday should give you plenty of ideas. Phone him when you feel well and truly aroused.

Tell him about the fantastic seduction you've planned for when he gets home. Describe in detail what you'll be wearing and what you're going to do to him. It will probably be a rather one-sided conversation because he'll be surrounded by people but half the fun is that only you and he know what you're saying. Keep in the mood until he gets home and you should have an evening to remember.

KEEPING IN TOUCH

If your partner is away from home you could phone in the evening, when he is getting ready for bed. Pamper yourself with a fragrant bubble bath and then dress in your sexiest underwear or night clothes. There may be no one to see you but if you look the part you are bound to feel more sexy. Phone your partner and tell him how much you are missing him and then describe in detail what you are wearing – don't be distracted into talking about family news, this call is just for the two of you.

Ask him what he's doing and then describe to him what you would do if he was there next to you. He'll probably be in bed but if he's not, get him to transfer the call to somewhere he won't be disturbed. It won't take him long to realize he's in for a raunchy time so just let your imagination run wild. Tell him the things he does to you which you really enjoy or ask him

◀ Let your fingers do the walking and your imagination run riot over the sizzling hot line...

to describe his favorite lovemaking scene: what exactly he would like you to wear and what he would like you to do to him. You may be in for some surprises. People who may be quite shy talking about sex face to face can really let themselves go over the phone.

By this stage you should both feel pretty passionate and you may not be able to resist caressing yourself. Don't be afraid to tell him precisely what you're doing – he's probably doing the same and what better way to ease the frustration of being apart than to orgasm to the sound of one another's voice?

Telephone sex even received the accolade of being made the subject of a major novel of the 1990s. In *Vox*, Nicholson Baker describes a long sexual telephone conversation between a man and a woman who build up a fantasy. Some critics thought the novel mere pornography, but many readers confessed to researchers that they found the idea of building up such a fantasy over the phone to be very sexually exciting.

ANYTIME, ANYWHERE?

Of course, with the increase in the use of portable phones, it's possible to contact your partner practically anywhere, anytime. Beware! It could cause a very embarrassing accident if you phoned him while he was driving and it's also a good idea to check your partner hasn't put his office phone on 'speaker' – you may find your sexy, loving words broadcast to his surprised, and envious, colleagues! ❤

KITCHEN CAPERS

Interrupt the drudgery of doing the dishes to create your own exciting 'kitchen sink' drama with some wild and spontaneous sex among the dirty dishes.

Spontaneous sex has an intensity and a power which all other lovemaking, however passionate, can sometimes lack. Such sex can take you by surprise and leave you feeling like you've run a marathon, and it has the delightful advantage of sending a shiver up your spine whenever you remember it in the days that follow.

IN THE MOOD FOR SEX

For the best ever spontaneous sex, the trick is for the initiating partner to coax his or her lover into the same mood with subtlety and speed, so that you are each on the same wavelength from the

▲ *Why wait? If you are both in the mood for making love, a dreary chore such as the dishes can so easily become a light-hearted game – and a springboard for scintillating spontaneous sex.*

▶ *Exchange your clothes for a layer of soapsuds as you both begin to bubble over with excitement!*

beginning. If you are both ready for love, you can take your partner to new heights of pleasure, enhanced by the unusual surroundings of a different place or room.

IN THE KITCHEN

One of the most exciting venues for spontaneous sex is the kitchen. After an evening's dinner party when all the guests have gone home and you are left to clear up the debris together; on a Sunday afternoon when all the family have been to lunch and departed; or simply after a romantic meal together – if you feel the urge, why wait until you are undressed in the bedroom?

If your lover is elbow-deep in soapsuds, approach with care. The gulf between housework and lovemaking is

that will leave them quivering like jelly, pleading for more.

FUN AND GAMES

There is endless scope for fun in the kitchen for those who like to play games when they make love. Start with the soapsuds in the sink and clothe your partner in bubbles – give them a hat, a bra, a codpiece or anything else you can think of. If the soapsuds start running out, make some more!

Food is another commodity at hand in the kitchen. Raid the refrigerator for goodies such as ice, whipped cream aerosols and yogurt, and treat your partner like dessert, spooning on the yogurt or cream and licking it off, while running the ice across nipples, earlobes and genitals. (Performing oral sex after having sucked an icecube is an equally delicious thrill.) Or go to the kitchen cupboard and turn your lover into a savory snack, using spreads, peanut butter or cream cheese.

THE KITCHEN TABLE

When it comes to penetration, be sure your love-making is not just an uncomfortable wriggle on a cold, hard surface.

If the passion and the urgency displayed by Jack Nicholson and Jessica

wide, but some may genuinely prefer to finish the first before starting the second. It is up to you to persuade them otherwise!

WINNING YOUR 'WICKED' WAY

Begin with a kiss on an erogenous zone such as the back of the neck – don't touch with your hands yet. Just explore the sensitive spot you have chosen with lips and tongue until you feel your partner soften and yield, then slide your arms around their waist, up to their chest or breasts and down to their genitals.

Free them from their clothes as quickly as you can. Slide your hands across their skin, seeking out the places that make them shiver at the touch of your fingertips. Treat them to everything you know they like best. Run your fingernails up and down their back, tease them with oral loveplay in places

▲ *Explore your partner's body with your hands, gliding over each and every sensuous curve.*

DOS AND DON'TS

DO REMEMBER TO DRAW THE BLINDS OR CURTAINS – YOU DON'T WANT TO PERFORM IN FRONT OF THE NEIGHBORS.

DO BEWARE OF ANYTHING HOT OR SHARP. OVENS, KETTLES AND CUTLERY CAN ALL CAUSE INJURY TO BARE SKIN.

DON'T MAKE LOVE WHILE COVERED IN SOAPSUDS . THEY CAN REDUCE THE EFFICACY OF A CONDOM AND CAN CAUSE IRRITATION IF THEY GET INSIDE THE VAGINA. SO IF YOU PLAY WITH THE BUBBLES ON YOUR BARE SKIN, RINSE WITH WARM WATER AFTERWARDS AND THEN RETIRE SOMEWHERE A LITTLE MORE COMFORTABLE TO MAKE LOVE.

energy while you lean up against them. When they are fully charged with the vibrations, begin penetration from whichever angle is the most comfortable.

THE KITCHEN CHAIR
The acrobats among you may want to use the kitchen chair as a prop. If you are not afraid of a cold seat, sit astride it and take your partner on your lap. She can push with her feet against the leg struts to get the rhythm going.

If that's not possible, rock backwards and forwards until you reach orgasm. Alternatively use the chair to perch on, and pull her towards you, this time facing outwards so that you can penetrate her from behind.

MOVING ON
However you like your quickies, make sure it's fun in the kitchen. If you or your partner find the surfaces too hard (you don't want to be covered in bruises) retire quickly to the living room or bedroom, and continue the fun in comfort. ❤

Lange in *The Postman Always Rings Twice* impressed you, try the same action on your partner.

Sweep her up and carry her to the kitchen table (but have a little forethought and take everything off first, don't sweep it off as in the film). Lay her back on the table top, penetrating her deeply from above. If the table is small, you can stand at the end while she lays back facing upwards, or she can bends across the table facing away from you as you take her from behind.

SEXY SURFACES FOR LOVEMAKING
Lift your partner on to a clear space and let her twine her legs around the small of your back. If the work surface is at the right height for you both, you can penetrate her simply by lifting her on to your penis while her buttocks rest on the kitchen top.

A great alternative is the washing machine or dishwasher. When switched on, the heat and vibrations generated can add a completely new sensation to your lovemaking. Sit your partner on a towel on the top of the machine and let them absorb the machine's pulsating

▲ ▼ As your excitement mounts, you can bring each other to the height of ecstasy with oral sex. A work surface or a sturdy kitchen table will provide the ideal platform for passion.

LOVE ON TAP

Turn your bathroom into a sensual playground, with erotic lighting, steamy water, scented oils and plenty of hot, wet passion.

In the years following the Crusaders' return to Europe, bath houses, which were inspired by the great Muslim pleasure palaces the soldiers had seen and enjoyed during their wars, started to reappear in the big towns and cities for the first time since the fall of the Roman Empire.

These bath houses, known as 'stews,' contained tubs designed to accommodate several people at a time. But bathing was not their only function. Operating also as brothels, they offered their clients more private tubs, where two could partake in ablutions in a comfortable horizontal position.

BATHROOM LOVE

Today's baths are rarely large enough to accommodate two people with ease. However, lovers with determination and a passion for water can transform their bathroom into a pleasure-seeker's paradise, with the help of a few props and a number of scented potions.

Whether it's a spontaneous quickie you're after – perhaps you're just preparing to go out for the night and you can't resist the curve of her stockinged thigh – or the result of premeditation – you visualize him covered in oil perched on the edge of the bath with you writhing in ecstasy on his lap – the bathroom can offer plenty in the way of action.

THE QUICKIE

Enthusiastics can make love in the bath, on the edge of the bath, on the mat on the floor, on the toilet or on the bidet (if

you have one). The bathroom offers endless scope for the inventive lover. With towel rails, basins, surfaces of all different heights and very little floor space, the classic missionary position is actually quite hard to achieve.

But the alternatives are endless: he can take her from behind, she can sit on his lap on the toilet or the edge of the bath, facing forward or away, they can make love standing in the shower; it all

▲ *Even if the bathroom is small it is still possible to make love in all kinds of different ways. Try the edge of the bath, facing the mirror so you can watch the enjoyment in your partner's face.*

may want to put some music on – place a cassette player outside the bathroom door and put a cassette on. (Don't plug it inside the bathroom because it may not be safe.)

To get yourselves in the mood and unwind, a glass of chilled champagne or sparkling wine makes a perfect aperitif to good lovemaking.

Start with sex in the rising steam. In any position you choose, anywhere in the bathroom except the bath, masturbate your partner in the sticky heat until you bring them to orgasm, then let them masturbate you.

Once you have achieved orgasm you can each slide into the bath, basking in the afterglow, while the warm scented water laps at your skin, enveloping you in fragrant waves. Don't fall asleep. You will miss out on what is to come.

depends on how fit you are and how far you are prepared to go.

And, of course, you can always take your partner by surprise and pull them into the water half-dressed. The way their wet clothes cling to the contours of their body should add an extra thrill to enhance your lovemaking.

WATERY DELIGHT

If you prefer a more conventional, pre-planned night of passion, undress each other while the bath is running and slip into comfortable robes. If the light is too harsh, bring candles in to the room – as many as you can find – place them all around the bath and light them.

Switch off the main light and watch the dancing shadows on the walls, floor and ceiling, and the glitter of their reflection in the water. Nothing enhances the form of the naked body better than candlelight.

Fill the bath with scented oil, foaming cream or bath salts to add fragrance to the water and soften your skin. You

▲ *Sit on your partner's knee. Dangle your feet in the warm, foaming bath water as you prepare for love.*

WET LOVE

When you have recovered your strength, arrange yourselves comfortably in the water and lather your partner all over with a rich, creamy soap, starting with the back and chest and finishing

▲ Kiss and caress her as she sinks into the bath. Lean over her, letting her enjoy her moment of captivity.

◄ She wraps her legs around his body. He balances her for comfort and deeper penetration. Keeping some clothes on can be erotic particularly if you're planning to get wet later!

it is just warm, then concentrate it on your partner's vulva. If your partner is sitting in the bath, hold the shower head under water and direct it towards her. Take care to position the spray so that it runs across her genitals, not actually up into her vagina.

Do the same with his penis and testicles, showering the warm water over the top and underneath, but make sure the water is not too hot.

LIP SERVICE

If there is room, you can take it in turns to perform oral sex while still in the water, bringing your partner almost to the point of orgasm.

When you have each had your turn, you can begin the actual penetration. The best position is for him to lay back in the water, while she eases herself down on top of his penis with her legs close together in a reversal of the classic missionary position. This way, you can bring each other to a slippery climax with very little effort at all.

For something a little more adventurous, she can sit on his penis, facing away from him and leaning slightly forward. The friction from the water should bring you both an exciting and different sensation at orgasm.

Continue your loving after the bath. Dry your partner sensuously after your bath and rub some light oil over their skin. Then start all over again. ❤

with the genitals. Work your fingers rhythmically around the sensitive parts and up into each secret place, gently stroking and sliding to explore every magical crease and fold.

When they can stand it no longer, shower them slowly clean with a giant sponge, dipped repeatedly in the warm water and squeezed out over their body. If you have a shower head attached to the taps or fixed over the bath, put it to good use. Run the water through it until

---

BATH GAMES

• CREATE GIANT BUBBLES WITH THE HELP OF FOAMING BATH OIL, SMOTHER EACH OTHER WITH GREAT HANDFULS, AND CREATE EROTIC SHAPES AND PICTURES.

• TURN THE LIGHTS OUT AND MAKE LOVE IN THE WATER IN DARKNESS. THE LACK OF VISION WILL HEIGHTEN THE OTHER SENSATIONS, GIVING GREATER PLEASURE.

• RUB YOUR PARTNER'S BODY WITH A LOOFAH TO GET THE SKIN TINGLING. EXPLORE THE DIFFERENT AND EXCITING SENSATIONS THE ROUGH BATH TOY PRODUCES.

GOOD CLEAN FUN!

Water is the essence of life itself - a cleanser, soother and healer - and an invigorating shower makes a perfect prelude to a sensual night with your lover.

▼ *The silky feel of wet, soapy skin against skin unleashes the natural sexual feeling in lovers.*

Personal hygiene is an essential requirement for good sex, and bathing is a wonderfully sensual and enjoyable aid to loving foreplay. With the help of exotic scented soaps and foaming gels, you can set the scene for a lingering night of lovemaking.

SHOWER POWER
Showers, by their design, are generally considered to be functional household appliances, but even the smallest cubicle can accommodate two people once they understand its limitations. Showers are particularly well-suited for most standing lovemaking positions (provided you are standing on a non-slip surface), but they can also be used as a sensual warm-up for further sex play.

Make your showertime an assault on the senses. Select your favorite music and play it. Meanwhile, both you and your partner can soap up and dance with your arms locked together, your bodies pressing against each other under the warm spray. You can set the tempo to match your mood, be it romantic or passionate.

A SOAKING SURPRISE
Introduce an element of surprise – take your lover's hand and pull them into the shower, partially clothed, as they arrive home from work. The struggle to get them free of wet clothing can be highly stimulating. But choose your moment – they won't appreciate having their best 'dry clean only' outfit soaked right

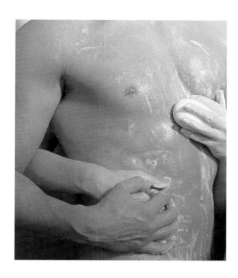

◄ *Use rich, scented soap to lather your partner's body. Work in slow, circular movements from the toes up to the neck. Pay special attention to the back and shoulders, then move on to the erogenous zones.*

through. Alternatively, climb in the shower yourself when your partner least expects it, wearing just a silky camisole or boxer shorts. Once it is wet, the fabric will cling seductively for a really stimulating effect.

The shower is also an ideal place for oral sex. The active partner can kneel on the shower floor with their head level with the other's penis or vulva, while the passive partner remains in a standing position.

SPECIALLY FOR MEN

Giving a man a shower can be an exciting way to bring him to the verge of orgasm. Make sure that the water is not too hot, then wash his back first and then his neck, splashing or spraying water on him throughout. Soap his front gently, lathering his chest, and slowly circle down towards his genitals. Then ask him to turn around and wash the backs of his legs and buttocks. Now, turn him around again and wash his testicles. Use featherlight strokes, keeping up a slow, but persistent pressure. Make a ritual of this, perhaps

◄ *The warm, tingling sensation of the shower spray can heat up the tempo when directed slowly up and down your lover's back.*

► *After a long hard day at work, pull him into the shower with you and slowly wrestle him out of his underwear.*

washing and rinsing his penis twice. Then bring him to the brink of ecstasy by using the slipperiness of the soap, simulate masturbation – but only as a teaser. After you have finished ignore any of his pleas to continue. Now it's your turn to enjoy the warm sensation of shower play.

▲ *Surprise him by joining him in the shower fully dressed. Wait until you are both wet, then let him peel off your clothes and underwear piece by piece.*

SPECIALLY FOR WOMEN

Women have an infinite variety of erogenous zones. Start by washing her hair using your fingers to rub in the shampoo and make the rinsing as sensuous an experience as you can. Scalp massage is invigorating at the best of times, but a lover's patient hands can add that extra tingling sensation. Encourage her to caress you as you lather, rinse and condition her hair, so you don't miss out on the fun too.

Play your soapy fingers right down her body until you reach the most pleasurable spots. Pay special attention to her breasts, spending as much time as you and she like – the French recognize this as a healthy way of maintaining good skin tone and shape as well as being undeniably erotic. Kiss her wet body all the time and press your body against her soapy back.

Save the rinsing of her genitals until last. Hold the shower attachment pointed towards her, cleansing her gently with a slow steady spray. Again, make sure it's not too hot, and take care not to direct the water right up into her vagina, as this can be dangerous.

AFTERGLOW

Once your shower play is over, rub each other dry with fluffy towels, working in slow, circular movements from top to toe. Complete by dusting your partner's body with lightly scented baby powder, or by massaging a palmful of rich moisturizing lotion into their skin. A deep massage will completely relax any tense and tired muscles.

To continue your lovemaking without breaking the mood, cover an exercise mat or cushions on the bathroom floor with soft towels and blankets. Turn up the heating so that the room is warm, pour yourself and your partner a drink, and let yourself go.　　♥

SHOWER DOS AND DON'TS

DO TEST YOUR SOAPS BEFORE USING THEM ON DELICATE GENITAL AREAS. THERE ARE MANY GOOD SOAPS AVAILABLE FOR SENSITIVE SKIN.

DO USE COLORFUL SHOWER SPONGE TOYS AND SOFT BODY BRUSHES TO GENTLY STIMULATE YOUR PARTNER.

DON'T MAKE THE WATER PRESSURE ON THE SHOWER HEAD TOO STRONG WHEN WASHING YOUR PARTNER'S GENITALS.

DON'T USE A RADIO OR PORTABLE CASSETTE RECORDER IN THE BATHROOM OR ANYWHERE NEAR WATER.

FUN WITH MIRRORS

Possibly the largest but least used sex aids in existence, mirrors can be found in every home, and when used creatively, can do more for your sex life than any number of aphrodisiacs.

▲ *Using mirrors during lovemaking allows you to watch your partner's body from new angles. By clever angling of several mirrors, you can see yourselves reflected many times over.*

Mirrors have always been surrounded by a certain mystique – there are countless myths and legends associated with them and their reflective powers.

Many millions of people spend many hundreds of hours dressing and preparing themselves in front of their mirrors, but how many think to use the mirror for undressing? The first-ever glimpse of yourself making love often comes as quite a shock. Whether you see

◀ Remember that the earth can move quite literally when you make love, so make sure that mirrors propped against furniture or on bedroom surfaces are secure and won't fall off.

▼▶ Just as watching people make love on film and video can be a great turn-on, so too can watching each other in mirrors. Lighting is all important, so use soft lamps or candles.

MIRROR MIRROR ON THE WALL

BEDROOMS DON'T ALWAYS LEND THEMSELVES TO BEING DECKED WITH MIRRORS – THERE IS OFTEN OTHER FURNITURE TO ACCOMMODATE. BUT IF YOU LIKE THE IDEA OF A LARGE MIRROR CLOSE TO THE BED, YOU COULD PUT ONE IN PLACE OF THE HEADBOARD. A LARGE MIRROR WITH AN ORNATE FRAME CAN FOLLOW THE TRADITIONAL CONTOURS OF THE HEADBOARD, OR FOR A MODERN ROOM, MIRROR TILES WILL DO JUST AS WELL. PILE UP PILLOWS AND CUSHIONS WHERE THE BED AND MIRROR MEET, AND YOU WILL HAVE ENHANCED THE ROOM DURING THE DAY IN ADDITION TO PROVIDING A SECRET SEXUAL AID FOR YOUR NIGHTS OF LOVE.

yourself and your partner in a hotel room mirror, or in the spare room of a friend's house, you might almost feel you have caught someone else in the act. However, those in the habit of seeing themselves performing sex together find that it can genuinely add a new dimension to their lovemaking.

FIRST REFLECTIONS
If you put up a mirror in your bedroom opposite the foot of the bed, or on the wall alongside, or better still if you have mirror closet doors, you can begin by simply watching yourselves make love. Just as dancers constantly observe themselves in mirrors to ensure that their posture and steps are correct, so too can you observe your position, and

yourself that only your lover sees. But, for other people watching their partner's body from new angles is the real pleasure. With many sexual positions, getting a good view of your partner is not easy. So much of the body is involved in the sexual act, and each bit undergoes its subtle change during the build up to orgasm that it is impossible to see and appreciate it all. Added to which, watching your partner's body move in time with yours can be extremely stimulating.

Using mirrors in the bedroom – or in any other room in which you choose to make love – can teach you so much more about one another and improve the harmony of your sexual technique.

If the sight of your naked reflection turns you off rather than on, then it might only take a small adjustment to change the way you feel about mirror sex. Just as in films, where it is all a question of clever camera angles and lighting, so it is in your own home, where high-powered and practical bedroom and bathroom lights show your skin in its full, blemished glory.

DIM THE LIGHTS

No one looks good under a stark fluorescent light or a 100 watt bulb, so try to tone it down a bit. Put in 40 watt bulbs or those that are tinted to gently color wash a room. Better still, try candles, the soft golden glow of which can give your bodies the gleam of an Old Master painting.

In the light of a few carefully-positioned candles, you can watch yourself writhe on honey-colored sheets, while the flickering flames create highlights and shadows on your bodies. In such unfamiliar light, your room can take on a strangely timeless feeling, and you can fantasize that you have been transported back into the past. ❤

improve your physical technique.

If you've ever wondered why sex never quite feels the way it looks in films, it's because the actors and actresses are playing to the camera. They know they are being watched, and what's more, most of the moves are choreographed – carefully set up to look as sexy as possible. Real sex rarely looks so slick, but watching yourself can help you tidy the edges. You can pretend that you are the heroine or hero, and give the sexual performance of your life. You will enjoy putting on an erotic visual display, and your partner will hopefully be turned on by the extra energy and power of your lovemaking.

Many people find such self-voyeurism fascinating. It reveals a part of

MOVING IN

The big day is here and you've got the keys to your dream home. Why not carry your partner across the threshold and christen your new residence with a good old-fashioned romp on the bare floorboards?

▶ *A provocative stance can bring something to mind that is sure to take some of the stress and strain away from what can be a very tiring day.*

▼ *During a break for coffee, sit behind your partner, nuzzle her neck and kiss her ears to make her aware that you really appreciate what she is doing for you.*

You know the feeling. A tingling sense of excitement invades your body from head to foot as the packing crates and the last bits of furniture are transferred from the moving van to your new living space. It's been hard work moving, but suddenly you feel

▲ *Slowly take off his pants but don't touch his flesh until it's obvious he knows what's on your inventive mind.*

▼ *After mouth-watering oral sex, straddle your partner and let him make love to you amid the debris of the day.*

exhilarated and eager as your helpful friends drive away with the truck and you are left alone with your lover at last.

Now is the perfect time to stop unpacking and 'move in' on your partner for some rough-and-ready sex among the boxes. A change of residence is a good time to make other changes, too. You can vow to make a new start to your sex life. Kick off on the right foot by making moving day a tasty day of sloppy fun and sweaty foreplay.

CASUAL SEDUCTION

Of course, you'll be wearing casual clothes in which you feel comfortable, but that doesn't mean you can't be sexy at the same time. Jeans are a time-honored sex symbol, and he should be wearing his sexiest pair, preferably the ones she likes best. Don a handsome shirt, with maybe a muscle-man T-shirt underneath. Silky boxer shorts are sexy and comfortable, so wear a pair for this special, informal occasion.

She can wear a well-worn pair of overalls, and perhaps an alluring body-suit which has snaps at the crotch for

DOS AND DON'TS

• DO POP OUT AND BUY A BAG OF ICE FOR A COOL CHANGE OF PACE. LINE THE FLOOR WITH PLASTIC, SCATTER THE ICE AND THEN MELT IT WITH THE HEAT OF YOUR LOVE-MAKING.

• DO REMEMBER TO PACK CONTRACEPTIVES WHERE YOU CAN GET THEM EASILY.

• DO MAKE SURE THE HOT WATER IS ON FOR A LIBIDO-LIBERATING SHOWER TOGETHER.

• DON'T STRIP OFF NEAR THE WINDOWS: THE NEIGHBORS MIGHT NOT APPRECIATE IT. YOU MAY NOT HAVE HAD TIME TO HANG CURTAINS, SO IMPROVISE WITH A TABLECLOTH.

◄ Now it's his turn to start to make her moving-in day one that she will remember for a long, long time.

▼ You both know that the room will have to be cleaned, but for now you have plenty of other things to do to keep you busy pleasurably.

easy access. Men love the ease with which they can unfasten and remove overalls and the sort of little-girl charm they imply. Be sure to wear a lacy bra for a sweet surprise, and some provocative panties. If you're feeling really wicked, wear nothing underneath apart from his favorite perfume.

IN THE MOOD FOR LOVE

Take advantage of a coffee break to give your partner a relaxing massage. This is the perfect opportunity for you to pounce on him while his eyes are shut, and have your wicked way ! Either take the subtle approach and straddle him fully clothed, then slowly and provocatively unzip his jeans, waiting for him to become excited before you touch his flesh. You can pull his pants off slowly, kissing his bare skin inch by inch as you do so, and then please him with a little tantalizing oral sex.

Or you may take the direct approach by ripping his pants off quickly, and then getting on top of him before he knows what has hit him. You can bend backwards and hold onto his legs, and then move forward and pull him up into sitting position, for a rocking intercourse motion. In either case, he will be more than happy to assist, making the earth move on a moving day you will both remember with a smile. ❤

150

PAINTPOT PASSION

Why not go in for a little house painting – it's one way of adding more than a lick of paint to your love life if it has become a bit dull, or even lackluster.

Have you ever enjoyed the fantasy that you have a charming and handsome painter in to paint your house, and you find yourself wondering just how hunky he is beneath his overalls, especially when he leans over to dip his brush into a paint can and you can see his firm, muscular buttocks clearly etched on his pants? Or, have you ever been up a ladder doing a little house painting totally bored with the repetitive up-and-down, up-and-down of the brush stroke when your partner comes into the room looking so desirable that you can't wait to drop the

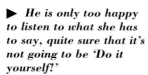

▲ *There must be a better way of passing the time than painting a room: and she has no qualms about suggesting just such a way!*

▶ *He is only too happy to listen to what she has to say, quite sure that it's not going to be 'Do it yourself!'*

◀ At this stage, why not use a soft, clean paintbrush to caress your partner's chest and again prove to him that it can be used for a lot of purposes other than applying paint.

▼ A securely placed ladder can be used to maneuver yourselves into a position that is full of potential for a couple willing to experiment with every aspect of love among the paintcans.

busy with a brush, come into the room, lean languidly against the ladder and give him the sort of look that brings the blood rushing to his cheeks – and the other parts of his body that you have your interior designs on!

STRIPPING

When he is safely earthbound, she takes the brush from his hand and runs it lazily over his face with one hand while unbuttoning his shirt with the other. When his chest is bared she teases him by running the silky bristles over his nipples and navel.

Now she takes her shirt off and uses the brush to caress her breasts until her nipples stand proud and tempting.

Meanwhile, the home handyman has taken off his jeans and uses his hands to prove to her that they can do more than wield a brush, while she uses the brush to bring him closer and closer to the

brush and let your hands go up and down somewhere completely different? Why not let your fantasies rip and get down to some serious sex among the paintpots? You'll be glad you tried it.

MAKING READY

And just as thorough preparation is the secret of successful painting, it's also the key to a skin-tingling, sensual experience that will leave a smile lingering on your lips for hours and hours after you are finished.

You don't need much. A dust sheet or two, a set of stepladders, some paintbrushes (the softer the bristles the better) and if you're really in the mood, some body paints. For him, a pair of overalls, or jeans and loose-fitting shirt to cover his modesty and the soft, silk boxer shorts he is wearing. And the same for her, only with a pair of really sexy panties.

Let him go up the ladder. When he is

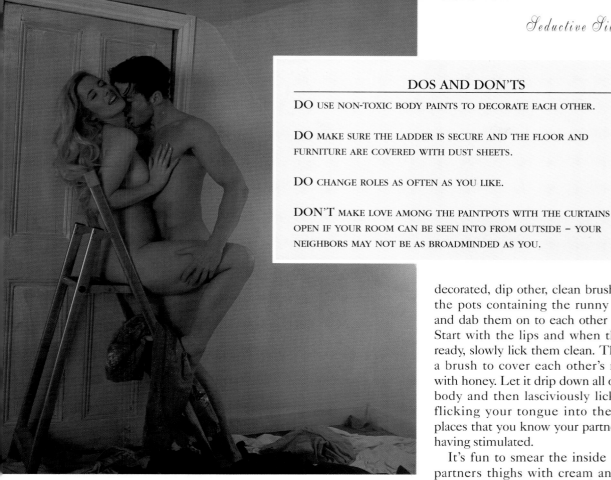

DOS AND DON'TS

DO USE NON-TOXIC BODY PAINTS TO DECORATE EACH OTHER.

DO MAKE SURE THE LADDER IS SECURE AND THE FLOOR AND FURNITURE ARE COVERED WITH DUST SHEETS.

DO CHANGE ROLES AS OFTEN AS YOU LIKE.

DON'T MAKE LOVE AMONG THE PAINTPOTS WITH THE CURTAINS OPEN IF YOUR ROOM CAN BE SEEN INTO FROM OUTSIDE – YOUR NEIGHBORS MAY NOT BE AS BROADMINDED AS YOU.

point where the room will be rocking so much that the paintcans will splash their contents on to the dustsheets!

FOOD FOR THOUGHT

And talking of the paintcans – that's where the added fun comes in. For while some are filled with non-toxic body paints, others could contain yogurt, syrup or other sweet, runny substances that are so sexy to roll around the mouth!

Use the body paint to gently decorate each other with whichever patterns come to mind. Having paint softly brushed on to your body, especially the erogenous regions, is a delightful experience – relaxing and yet at the same time arousingly stimulating.

When both your bodies are suitably

▲ *Who cares that there will be a little mess to clear up, the fun that you are both having will more than compensate for that.*

decorated, dip other, clean brushes into the pots containing the runny liquids and dab them on to each other as well. Start with the lips and when they are ready, slowly lick them clean. Then use a brush to cover each other's nipples with honey. Let it drip down all over the body and then lasciviously lick it off, flicking your tongue into the secret places that you know your partner loves having stimulated.

It's fun to smear the inside of your partners thighs with cream and even better fun for him or her when you tongue it off, for you both know that it is sure to lead to a sizzling oral sex session.

PAINTING PASSION

If you want it to end there, that's up to you, but if you can control your climax continue to drive each other wild with your tantalizing brush technique. After that it's up to you which position to adopt for full-scale penetrative sex. Whichever one you decide on, and you've come this far so you may as well be as adventurous as you possibly can, as long as it is mutually pleasurable, do what you can to draw it out, remembering to give as much pleasure as you are getting.

And remember, nowadays, its not just men who are decorators – there's nothing to stop the woman being up the ladder and the man playing seducer! ❤

$\mathscr{S}$HEDDING INHIBITIONS

Some of the most unlikely places can make perfect sex hideaways, and one such is the humble garden shed. Crammed with lawn mowers and flowerpots it creates an unusual backdrop for some exciting quickie sex.

◀ *Whether you love or loathe gardening, you may never view it in the same light again once you 'shed' your inhibitions.*

▶ *Surprise your partner by planting a big kiss that's sure to grow into something more exciting. It may be a good idea to prune some clothing – but not too much as you may be overlooked.*

▼ *Having sown the seeds of passion, now's the time to find a secret hide-away. How about the garden shed?*

A good sex life takes imagination and a genuine willingness on the part of each partner to try new things. New things can mean new places, and even the most unlikely venue can add a bit of spice to your lovemaking – or at least give you something to laugh about later!

A SEXY HIDE-AWAY

There are relatively few places close to home where you can hide away from kids, pets and neighbors and even parents, but one such is the garden shed. Often crowded with gardening implements, toys and old boxes, festooned with cobwebs and crawling with insects, it rarely offers much in the way of space

insect population, and so long as neither of you has a real spider phobia, it's best to leave them alone.

The position you choose for sex will depend on the space you have. A standing position is by far the easiest, and depending on the cleanliness of the shed, you may not want to sit on a bench or lay on the floor. Use whatever is at hand to steady you – an old chair, a bicycle, lawn-mower handles or an old shelf.

If you know there is no danger of you being disturbed, remove all your clothes. You can face each other, she wrapping her legs around his back and he lifting her on to his penis. If you are of unequal height, this takes some strength, but is great for a quickie. Otherwise he can take her from behind, so long as she has the space to bend over slightly. It will be just like playing hide and seek as children, but a million times better.

SHED SURPRISE

If you want to take your partner by surprise, you will either have to pounce while they are actually working in the shed, or make some excuse for them to join you there. Either way it is up to you to lure them in to your den. If the shed is large enough you may be able to make some rough preparations such as

▲ *Most garden sheds offer limited space. But this need not detract from your pleasure as long as you have removed any sharp items.*

and comfort. However it can be surprisingly exciting, and the dry, dusty odor of cedarwood, creosote, old canvas and potting compost could even become quite an aphrodisiac if you make a quickie in the shed a habit.

GARDEN ADVENTURE

If you and your partner are accustomed to trying new places, prepare yourselves for your adventure beforehand. You can start by removing your underwear before heading into the backyard. With your top clothes on, nobody will notice the difference, and you will have less clothing to struggle out of when the time comes.

Once inside the shed, have a quick look around you for hazards – make sure there is nothing sharp or dangerous which you could fall on or hit accidentally in the heat of the moment. There is little you can do about the shed's

DOS AND DON'TS

DO MAKE SURE THAT YOU REMOVE ALL SHARP OBJECTS AND INSTRUMENTS FROM YOUR GARDEN SHED BEFORE LURING YOUR PARTNER INTO YOUR SECRET, SEXY HIDE-AWAY.

DO MAKE SURE THAT YOUR PARTNER IS NOT CLAUSTROPHOBIC!

DON'T GET CARRIED AWAY AND 'PRUNE' TOO MANY CLOTHES BEFORE YOU RETREAT INTO THE PRIVACY OF THE GARDEN SHED.

DON'T FEEL LEFT OUT IF YOU HAVEN'T GOT A GARDEN SHED. YOU CAN ALWAYS IMPROVISE: AN ATTIC, CELLAR – OR EVEN A CLOSET

laying out a rug or setting up a garden chair. Those with a huge amount of space can even put up a chaise lounge. But beware! They are not designed for heavy athletics.

Once inside, shut the door and wedge it so that they can't escape – if they are still unsuspecting of your motives, make it clear with a big kiss on the lips. Give them the sexiest kiss imaginable, one that cannot fail to turn them on. Slide your arms about them to still any final protest and run your hands over their erogenous zones down to the penis or clitoris. If there is room, you can perform oral sex, kneeling while your partner stands. Otherwise bring them slowly to the point of orgasm by hand. Your partner may never look upon gardening or home repair in the same light again.

Greenhouse

If you have a greenhouse, sex among the plants can be another thrill. Barely hidden by the lush greenery of tomato plants, geraniums or fuchsias, there is the added danger that someone might glimpse you through the glass. Let the thick, heady scent of the foliage transport you to hotter climes – you might be

▲ ▼ The close confines of the garden shed may limit your choice of positions but not your fun. Now you can discard all your clothes, make love sitting astride your partner or, if there's room, kiss and caress each other and then indulge in oral sex.

in a jungle or on a tropical island. Either way, the sensual heat in the height of summer will tempt you to linger longer beneath the glassy sky and take your time with your lovemaking.

What is certain is that wherever you choose to make love, the scents and smells of those strange surroundings will always make you smile when you catch a whiff of them in the future.

Above and Below

Garden sheds are just one of a number of secret places you can make love with your partner. Attics and cellars are equally exciting for those who are prepared to brave the dust, spiders, old suitcases and cardboard boxes.

Crawl into the attic in a rainstorm, and hear the pounding of the raindrops on the roof, or escape into the cellar for some speedy, sensual sex where nobody can find you. If others are in the house, it may even add to the excitement to know that people are so close, and have no idea where you are and what you are doing. ♥

AL FRESCO FUN

The summer is a wonderful time for love, so surprise your partner with a sumptuous picnic and make the most of this warm, sensuous season.

There are few things like the joys of nature to bring out the natural instinct in lovers. A hot, balmy day, white clouds floating in the summer sky and a gentle breeze ruffling the leaves of lush green trees combine to give summer a rich sensuality quite unlike any other season.

A picnic on such a day is the perfect aphrodisiac for lovers whose sexual palates have become jaded with the constant round of work, household chores and family duties.

If you have children, send them to their friends for the day (you can do the same for their parents later) and prepare yourselves for a wonderful, erotic day in the country.

PEACE AND TRANQUILLITY
Your eventual destination can make or break the picnic. Great beauty spots tend to attract crowds on a warm day, so head for somewhere a little off the beaten track. It is worth an extra 20 minutes' walk or drive for some genuine peace, even if it does seem a tremendous effort at the time. Alternatively, if you know of a lovely place really close to you, why go farther? And those with secluded, woody back yards may not want to move away from home at all.

THE PICNIC HAMPER
However, if you are planning to walk some distance, don't overpack the picnic hamper, as once you get there you may find that you are hungry for little else but love. Simple things are best – a bottle of good wine – if you have a cool bag you can have chilled white wine and a bottle of mineral water – French bread, some Brie and ham, followed by a basket of juicy ripe peaches, fresh strawberries or crisp pears.

Just as important is the presentation. Take wine glasses, a picnic cloth, napkins and an umbrella (as a sunshade, but you never know) to give a real celebratory feel to the day.

AN AFTERNOON IDYLL
A leisurely lunch of delicious, French-style food, coupled with the mild aphro-

▼ It doesn't matter what sort of food you have made for your picnic; it will probably be low on your list of priorities once you and your partner have found yourselves a suitably isolated spot.

DOS AND DON'TS

• BEWARE OF CIGARETTES AS THEY CAN CAUSE FIRES AND ALWAYS TAKE YOUR RUBBISH HOME WITH YOU (THAT INCLUDES CONDOMS WHICH, ONCE DISCARDED, ARE A DANGER TO WILDLIFE).

• DO REMEMBER THAT LOVEMAKING IN A PUBLIC PLACE IS ILLEGAL – USE YOUR INITIATIVE AND BE DISCREET.

• DON'T WORRY IF YOUR PICNIC SPOT IS CROWDED – ENJOY YOUR MEAL THEN MAKE LOVE IN PEACE ONCE YOU GET BACK HOME.

disiac of a glass of fine wine will almost certainly put you in the mood for love, and now you have nothing left to do but devote the rest of the day to each other.

Lay close to one another and close your eyes, let the warmth of the sun caress your skin, and breathe in the heady fragrance of the cool sweet grass mingled with the familiar smell of your partner's body. If you have chosen a shady spot, remove your partner's shirt or T-shirt and watch the dappled light play on his warm smooth skin.

Even if you set out well covered in suntan lotion, it won't hurt to apply another layer. Give each other a sun lotion massage – there is nothing more guaranteed to turn your partner on in the summer heat.

Let him lie on his front and trace patterns on his back with a twig. Spell out his name, your name and follow this with secret messages. Only refill his glass with wine if he can guess what they are.

For him, pluck a leaf and explore her erogenous zones. Stroke the earlobes, the soft line of the upper lip, the neck and the chest. Blindfold her with a scarf

▲ *However secluded the spot, it is always best to wear the sort of clothes that are designed to make love in! You don't want to get caught in the buff by the local hikers! But don't let being clothed spoil your pleasure; fondling can be lots of fun.*

▶ *The fresh air, coupled with good food and fine wine, can be a great aphrodisiac – and, as long as you are assured complete privacy, you can let yourself go with abandon.*

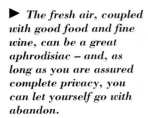

and ask her to guess what it is you're using to tickle her back. A pine cone, a single blade of grass, a meadow flower or a down-covered dandelion. Take inspiration from the things you find around you.

CHILDHOOD PLEASURES

Revert to simple childhood pleasures and make daisy chains; find buttercups or other small yellow flowers and hold them under the chin – the reflection proves that your lover has a passion for butter; and blow the seeds from dandelions as you make wishes. You could even try pulling the petals from a flower to find out whether 'He loves me' or 'He loves me not.' If you sus-

▶ *Bathed in warm sunshine, you can luxuriate in the afterglow of lovemaking. A blade of grass, a soft flower petal – or whatever you have at hand – can be used to lovingly stroke and relax your partner.*

pect 'He loves me not' then cheat with the last few petals!

AS BARE AS YOU DARE

Undress as much as you dare, but remember that hikers and curious children can seek out lovers in the most secret of places.

If she has come prepared, wearing a loose, voluminous skirt, he can slide his hand up into the soft regions of her thighs, lingering on the aspect of pleasure and caressing her sensitive skin with a plucked flower head. Tickle her until she cries out for mercy, or until she slides her own hand into the fly of your jeans, making you groan with desire.

Thus hidden by long grass, thick bushes or a clump of trees, you can make love to the sound of the wind rustling in the leaves. Let your inhibitions drift away with the summer breeze and enjoy the warm sensation of the sun on your skin, the hard earth beneath you and the deep blue eternity of the sky above. Take in all there is of the nature around you as you climax with your lover, and feel truly at one with the earth. ❤

𝒫ATIO PASSION

Enjoy an afternoon of passion on a warm sunny day in the privacy of your own secluded patio or terrace. Follow a few simple guidelines and you'll have only the birds and bees to think about!

On a lazy summer afternoon there is nothing better than spending a few hours relaxing on the patio or terrace with a good book or a pile of Sunday papers.

In the leafy seclusion of your own home, you know that you will not be disturbed. Tall fences shield you from the nosy neighbors and the surrounding trees, in full leaf, provide an impenetrable wall between yourselves and passers-by.

Suddenly, you want to make love.

◀▲ *Sitting with your partner in the seclusion of your patio, terrace or garden, you may well get the urge to turn up the heat. It shouldn't be long before he gets the message that patio passion is what you have in mind. Wear something that is cool, loose and won't get in the way as temperatures soar!*

You know you can't wait, nor do you need to go inside the house, for in the perfect privacy of your secluded patio, there are no onlookers but the birds and the bees.

SUBTLE SEDUCTION
Whatever the weather, you may want to turn up the heat! But approach your partner with care, for sex in the afternoon might be the last thing on their mind if they are dozing lightly in the sun. Try awakening their passion with some gentle foreplay. You know what gets them going, but a soft, seductive approach may well surprise them into action immediately.

Start with a fresh application of suncream, gently massaging all exposed areas. Begin with the feet – an exceptionally erotic area for many – and work slowly up the calves to the thighs. Or concentrate on the hands and arms, caressing the inner sides from the wrists to the elbows with your fingertips.

Blow gently into their ears, nibbling the soft lobes with your lips and kissing the hairline from the back of the neck all the way round to the forehead. By now you should have awakened their desires. You will both be yearning

▲ *Take your time over some gentle foreplay and let him concentrate on your most 'get-at-able' erogenous zones.*

for more and, as long as you have taken adequate precautions with regard to privacy, get ready to jump on the patio passion wagon.

DIFFERENT POSITIONS
Outdoor sex can have an entirely different, intense flavor from that which you are accustomed to in bed. To begin with, the traditional missionary position is all but impossible, surrounded as you are with only the hard surfaces of the paved ground and canvas garden chairs. (You could, of course, try it on a chaise lounge, but they are not always sturdy enough.)

Better to use your imagination with what is around you. He can lift her on to his lap, while balancing on the edge of the garden table, or lay her gently backward over the table, while he remains standing at the end. Or if you prefer the eroticism of the rear-entry position, she

SENSUAL SECLUSION
IF YOU ARE WORRIED ABOUT NOSY NEIGHBORS WATCHING YOUR EVERY MOVE, YOU CAN CREATE YOUR OWN PRIVATE LEAFY LOVE NEST ON YOUR PATIO WITH VERY LITTLE EFFORT AND EXPENSE.

SECTIONS OF TRELLIS COVERED WITH FAST-GROWING CREEPERS SUCH AS VIRGINIA CREEPER OR CLEMATIS WILL GIVE YOU AN EFFECTIVE SCREEN IN JUST ONE SEASON.

PERGOLAS HELP SHIELD YOU FROM PRYING EYES ABOVE, IN ADDITION TO PROVIDING WELCOME SHADE IN A WARM SPOT. YOU CAN CONSTRUCT ONE FROM A DOZEN SIMPLE LENGTHS OF WOOD AND A HANDFUL OF NAILS, SETTING THE FOUR UPRIGHTS IN TUBS OF CONCRETE, IF YOU DON'T WANT TO DIG INTO THE GROUND.

THE FINAL, SIMPLEST METHOD OF ENSURING COMPLETE PRIVACY IS TO HANG SHEETS AROUND THE EDGE OF A LARGE GARDEN UMBRELLA, CREATING AN ARABIAN-STYLE TENT, FOR ALL YOUR DESERT SHEIK FANTASIES.

can bend forwards, supporting herself on a sturdy garden chair, or even a tub of flowers while you caress her buttocks through her flimsy summer clothes.

If you have a patio swing, or swing seat, this could add a whole new dimension to your lovemaking – she can sit astride him while the swing rocks gently to and fro. You will both feel like you're flying as you climax in mid-air.

FLIGHTS OF FANCY

Combine physical inventiveness with inventiveness of a different kind. Let the experience of making love out of doors take you back to your last vacation in the sun, where you made love on the balcony or roof to the sound of the

▲ The positions you choose for making love will be largely determined by the sort of garden furniture you have and how strong it is. A sturdy garden table could make a suitable impromptu bed – otherwise use your imagination.

distant waves on the beach, and sipped cool margaritas to quench your thirst in the afterglow.

Alternatively let your fantasies transport you: she can indulge in passionate foreplay with a young, muscular gardener; he can be a plantation owner teaching his young lover the joys of sex.

FOLLOW YOUR INSTINCTS

If you are still wary of making love out of doors, there is no need to deprive yourselves of the pleasure; just keep all of your clothes on, loosening only what is really necessary.

Such quickie sex can prove to be just as erotic, if not more so – you are following your natural urges when they strike – and with a partially-clothed partner, you can enjoy the pleasure of watching fabric against skin, and feeling a warm, ripe body through thin summer garments.

When you have finished making love, there will be no frantic rush to put your clothes on again should anyone drop by; instead you can resume your quiet pastime of reading for the rest of the afternoon. ❤

◀ Now's the time to return the compliment and lavish some attention on your partner.

THE BACK SEAT

Drive your partner to the brink of ecstasy by suggesting some sexy play in your car. Pull off the road and into your driveway or garage, and abandon yourself when the urge for lovemaking takes you.

▲ *For many people, the car is the ultimate sex symbol – an unconscious phallic symbol, representing both social standing and sexual prowess. Take a detour to a secluded spot and find out why.*

As you drive down the road, why not put the thought of sexy play into your partner's mind by lightly stroking his or her leg in a gentle way so that you will not distract either your or your partner's attention from safe driving.

Then, if your subtle suggestions get the green light, head for your own drive-way or garage. If you live in the country and it is evening, you may be able to find a secluded spot where you know you will not be seen. Remember that public sex is against the law.

If privacy is a problem, passionate kissing is always a good prelude to love-making, and sometimes it can be just as

163

DOS AND DON'TS

DO FORGET TO WEAR UNDERWEAR WHEN YOU ARE PLANNING TO SURPRISE YOUR PARTNER WITH A FLIRTATIOUS CRUISE IN THE CAR.

DO PRETEND THAT YOU ARE IN YOUR FAVORITE EXOTIC FOREIGN LOCATION, EVEN IF YOU ARE PARKED IN YOUR OWN DRIVEWAY.

DON'T SCRAPE YOUR LEGS ON STICK SHIFTS OR SHARP METAL EDGES ON SEATS – IT COULD BE A MAJOR PASSION KILLER! BE AWARE OF HOW MUCH SPACE YOU HAVE IN WHICH TO MANEUVER.

DON'T TRY TO PERFORM ORAL SEX WHILE ONE OF YOU IS DRIVING AS THIS CAN BE HIGHLY DANGEROUS.

DON'T HAVE SEX IN THE CAR IN BROAD DAYLIGHT IN FULL VIEW OF THE NEIGHBORS.

satisfying as genital contact. Make the most of deep, luscious mouth-to-mouth kisses before moving on to further caressing and foreplay. Nibble your partner's ears and neck, then – if you are in a secluded spot – unbutton the top of their shirt and lick down their chest or cleavage and prepare for a drive into ecstasy.

SHIFT INTO FIRST GEAR

Rev up the amorous engine by fondling your partner in a more obvious manner. Rub your hand up and down their trouser legs or skirt, while still clothed. Bite the insides of their thighs. Put your head in their lap and simulate oral sex through their clothes. It is quite easy to perform oral sex on a man who is sitting upright, but you can playfully tease him to build up excitement.

▲ *In the right setting the car makes an ideal place for intimate, spontaneous sex. It is a safe space which is enclosed, yet you are still 'outside' and so may experience the thrilling feeling of possibly being watched or caught in the act.*

▶ *After some initial fondling, you'll both be ready for some sizzling sex. The woman can sit astride her lover with her back to him. And instead of being a restriction, the car seat in front can give extra leverage for exciting rear-entry lovemaking.*

► *The man can move around into the classic 'doggie' position, which will give him greater control of movement and depth of penetration.*

While remaining in the front seat, the woman may straddle her lover after removing her skirt or pants. The man can simply unzip his fly and pull his trousers open to be instantly ready for action. She can put her arms around his neck or hold on to the back of the seat for support, and he can hold her waist, while she moves up and down on top of him.

BACK SEAT BOOGIE

For a really sizzling and sexy session, climb into the back seat of the car and tear off each other's clothes. In man-on-top positions, the woman can place one leg across the top back of the front seat, and prop one leg against the back window shelf. The man can give the woman oral sex, or penetrate her deeply in this position.

If you have reclining seats, the scope for movement can be greater. The woman can get on top facing the man, or mount him with her back to him if she is careful about where she places her legs. The thrill of intercourse in a limited space can make orgasm that much more intense. ❤

EASY RIDER!

What does your lover get up to while he's tinkering with his motorbike in the garage? What better way to find out than by seducing him on it – and enjoying some high-powered sex.

Motorbikes are considered by many people to be the most erotic two-wheeled creation in the world. The soft leather saddle, the sleek lines of the metal body, the throaty roar of the motorbike's ignition and the pulsing power of the engine all combine to produce a machine which over the years has transcended all others as a symbol of sex and freedom.

FAST AND FURIOUS

But it is not just the motorbike itself that projects a sexual message. Speed is an aphrodisiac, and a fast ride on an open road, coupled with the proximity of the leather-clad pillion passenger, is a certain recipe for arousal of the most passionate kind.

TAKE A TRIP

For the majority of us, the ultimate 'biker' encounter would, perhaps, take place on a moonlit summer night after a long ride, on the shore of a deserted lake, where you can gaze into the star-spangled heavens while making love to your partner on the still-warm tank of the motorbike. But such opportunities are rare, of course, and most people have to seize this type of sexual moment a little closer to home.

JOURNEY'S END

The garage itself, even though at first glance it might not seem a very sexy place, is perfect. Sheltered and private, you can pull in at your journey's end or

▶ *Tearing your lover away from his bike may prove difficult at first, but the reward is an encounter full of passion.*

▼ *Once you are 'on board' his bike, tease your man with kisses and caresses while he runs his hands over your body.*

◄ *Use your imagination to try out all sorts of positions in a new and exciting way. Amaze your lover by getting him to drape himself across the warm leather of his bike while you perform oral sex on him.*

work. Start by sliding provocatively back and forth on the leather saddle to adjust your position. Then, with your partner watching, begin a slow, languorous striptease, easing yourself as sexily as you can out of your clothes until you are on the bike saddle in nothing but your underwear.

Let him come to you and, as he does so, spin round to sit side-saddle, wrapping your legs around his waist, and running your fingers up and down his spine. Kiss his lips, nibble his earlobes and breathe hot passionate words into his ears.

DIRTY SEX

His hands may be dirty, but don't back off – let him cover you with his greasy fingers, touching your face, your breasts, your thighs, until you are dirtier than he is. Hold him tightly, writhing under his oily touch until he succumbs, and starts

creep down together during the night to fulfil your fantasies across the wide leather seat. The unusual location can even add to the excitement – and perhaps enable you to escape the confines of the house, with its ever-present children or parents.

THE MECHANICS OF SEDUCTION

If your partner is more interested in cleaning and tuning his bike than making love on it, and has never considered that his bike could be a double source of pleasure, he may need a little coaxing.

Next time he disappears into the garage to start work, follow him. You can do so on an innocent pretext – by fetching him a cup of tea, coffee or a cold beer, for example. Stay while he finishes the drink, wandering around the machine, admiring its sleek form, remarking on its power. Check that it is safely on its stand, then swing your legs astride it, trying it for size.

TACTICS

Once on the bike your seduction tactics will have to be obvious, or he may think you are just getting in the way of his

▼ *While you are lying prone get your man to mount his bike and enter you while sitting up.*

to remove his own clothing.

While he undresses, lay back on the tank and slide your fingers into your panties and down towards your clitoris. Masturbate in front of him until he is hard and erect, then let him straddle the bike as if he were about to ride it.

With his body leaning forward over yours, his hands clutching the rubber handle grips, guide his penis into you. Then, with your legs twined around his back, and your hands on his shoulders, you can start to move slowly in time with one another.

POLE POSITIONS

As he is in the riding position, he will have the pleasure of watching you both reflected in the chrome of the handle-bars and in the bike's mirrors.

Of course, you can change position – sitting face to face or with the woman on top, but any change should be effected carefully so as not to rock the bike.

GATHERING SPEED

If you dream of actually riding the motorbike while making love, go for the next best thing and adopt a position that's closer to your fantasy.

Let him sit astride the bike as if he were about to start it, then climb on in

▲ *The woman-on-top position works well on a bike too! If you fantasize about speed, this can be highly fulfilling.*

front of him, gently lowering yourself down on to his penis. Lean forward and grasp the handle grips, then find the foot rests with your feet. Once you are both comfortable, start to flex your knees up and down and give your lover, riding behind you, the trip of his life.

GARAGE LOVE

If the garage is spacious and all but empty, an extraordinary orgasm awaits. If the walls resound slightly to your spoken word, they will echo to your cries as you climax, amplifying and scattering your pleasure about the four walls.

When you have recovered your breath, the well-organized seductress will lead her partner back into the house and into a deliciously hot shower, where you can slowly and sensuously wash all the dirt and grease from each other's bodies. ❤

DOS AND DON'TS

DON'T BE TEMPTED TO HAVE THE BIKE RUNNING WHILE YOU MAKE LOVE IN AN ENCLOSED GARAGE – YOU COULD BE OVERCOME BY THE FUMES AND BE DISCOVERED *IN FLAGRANTE DELICTO* BY NEIGHBORS!

DON'T GET OVER-EXCITED AND ROCK THE BIKE OFF ITS STAND – ALTERNATIVELY, MAKE DOUBLE SURE IT IS STABLE BEFORE YOU START.

DO BE CAREFUL NOT TO GET ENGINE OIL, DIRT OR GREASE FROM DIRTY HANDS ON TO ANY SENSITIVE PARTS OF YOUR BODY.

DO TAKE YOUR FANTASY AS FAR AS YOU CAN. IF YOU WANT TO DRESS UP IN FULL BIKE LEATHERS, GO AHEAD. IT COULD INCREASE THE FUN.

SEX IN THE OFFICE

It might not seem it at first glance, but passion may be lurking among the filing cabinets. Take care not to overplay your hand and you should keep your job as well as your love.

There is something very erotic about men and women being thrown together every working day in an office – but the last thing that's supposed to be on your mind is sex. Because it is (usually) an off-limits subject, it can easily become an obsession. If you can't have it, you usually want it all the more.

Just because you're supposed to have an affair with your computer and nothing else during office hours, your eye will tend to alight on the interesting bulge in a man's trousers, or on a good pair of legs. Doing something about it is something else entirely – you don't want to be accused of sexual harassment! So what are the chances of having sex in the office?

▶ *Desktop dalliances can result in more than just raised eyebrows.*

▼ *Office passion can be just the explosion your sex life needs. Don't hold back, let it out...slowly.*

up half-naked under the desk (and under the marketing manager). But there are usually secluded spots even in the busiest office building – such as empty offices and stationery closets, and if all else fails the nooks and crannies of a fire escape can provide adequate shelter and privacy.

OVERTIME

Staying late together is another good way of being able to use the office space for sex play, although you'll have to keep an eye open for security guards and janitors. Make sure you don't tell too many people that you're staying late when the others leave – they might want to know where all your extra work has disappeared to the next day.

Unless you have an iron back and a passion so great that you don't mind being practically impaled on paperclips and shredders, the actual sex is likely to be what used to be called 'knee-tremblers' – you do it standing up, the woman usually supporting her back against the wall. This has its drawbacks – foreplay will often be

The only time your colleagues are likely to turn a blind eye to anything from French kissing to almost complete penetrative sex is at the office party. At Christmas it's traditional for everyone to lose their inhibitions after a few drinks, and to find expression (at last) for those secret desires they have been harboring all year long.

Couples often prove ingenious when it comes to finding places to indulge in a spot of heavy petting – full sex under desks is not unknown.

Of course you are not likely to have sex in the middle of the office on a wet Monday afternoon, no matter how much you might want it. And if you do try it, you can kiss your job goodbye with immediate effect! But people can and do have sex in office situations – the very risk of being discovered adds to the overall sense of excitement you feel. It's just like having sex in any other sort of public place (a park, for example) except that this one carries the risk of being caught by your boss.

Unlike at the office party, you can't throw caution to the winds and end

▲ *An empty desk with rising temperatures and only each other to stare at.*

▼ *Maintaining each other's attention in a small space shouldn't be too difficult.*

minimal and unless you are both much the same height the man's penis may not sit comfortably in his lover's vagina. If he is strong, he can lift the woman up slightly so that she is almost straddling him, but he won't be able to keep this up for very long.

BLANKETS

Lying on the floor is better, but can be very hard on whoever is underneath: throwing a couple of coats down first makes an adequate blanket – be careful not to get them stained.

In this type of situation it's often a better idea not to have full sex, but to bring each other to orgasm through mutual masturbation or to have oral sex. It's just as satisfying and less of a strain on the back.

Sex in the office is essentially about passion – it may also involve love, but if it is going to develop into a lasting relationship then you will have to find somewhere more comfortable and romantic for your sex, whether your lover is single or married. If the latter, it is not a good idea to have sex where you can be seen.

▶ *Late nights slaving over a hot computer could turn into a serious work habit.*

▼ *Privacy's difficult to find, but essential once you've passed the point of no return.*

Grappling with your passion among the computers is wild and should be fun, but it may only happen once. If it becomes a regular occurrence and is your only form of sex then not only are you running an increasing risk of being caught and putting your job at risk, but you are allowing it to prevent you from enjoying the kind of really satisfying sex that you deserve. ❤

SLEEPY-TIME SEX

*When you're both busy, making love is often a
'last-thing-at-night' activity. Sleepy-time sex, however, has its
own attractions and can often be surprisingly satisfying.*

▲ **End of the day
relaxation often has a
wonderfully
aphrodisiacal
quality.**

Sexual relationships tend to begin energetically. When you've only just met, you might spend long afternoons – perhaps even whole days – in bed, indulging in the most creative and athletic sort of lovemaking. As you get used to each other, however, and perhaps start living together, more practical considerations get in the way and the tendency is to make love only last thing at night when you are both tired out.

When you're working or looking after small children stress can mount. What you really need is a long vacation, but all you have is those precious few moments before you go to sleep.

THE MAGIC HOURS
Managing to have sex at this time is considerably better than having no sex at all. Although one of you may

Lying together in your own bed in your own space and feeling drowsy, is the time to enjoy all those little erotic caresses that your more athletic love-making might neglect. Kissing and nuzzling each other's ears, brushing a bare shoulder with your tongue, stroking hair and caressing very gently any part of your partner's body that comes easily to hand – all these relatively small gestures of love and desire culminate in a heady sense of growing sexual pleasure.

You may not want to move very much – sleepy-time sex can have an almost hypnotic effect – and so lying in a position where you can easily masturbate each other gently will avoid the necessity of having to jump about and wake yourselves up completely. You might like to take turns – facing slightly toward each other means you can easily reach the vulva or penis, although the one being touched might prefer to lie flat.

end up feeling cheated if it is the only time you ever have sex, making love just before you go to sleep, or as you are waking in the morning, can help to reinforce all the good things about your relationship and provide a welcome release from tension.

There is a particular erotic and magical quality about the hours when no one else is stirring, when there is only the ticking of the clock to remind you of the world outside. There are no children causing havoc, no phones ringing, no problems to be solved. The only thing that matters is enjoying each other and having the best orgasm possible. Lying in each other's arms as you go to sleep has its own special kind of intimacy – one that, far from diminishing over the years, actually grows.

AN EROTIC TIME

It may seem unlikely that wearing your old nightie or pyjamas is going to be a great turn-on, but there is something especially sexy about a desirable body clad in such prosaic garments. There can be something very comforting about the very innocent feel of good old flannel!

▲ *Caresses when you are either half-asleep or half-awake are very intimate.*

▼ *Morning sex, after a night cuddled up together, can be very exciting.*

Lying in the 'spoons' position, that is side by side with the woman 'sitting' on the man's lap as they curl into one another, means that he can enter her from behind with very little extra movement, and she can control the pace and strength of his thrusting with the minimum of effort. In this position the man can fondle his partner's breasts while kissing the back of her neck and ears – and once you have come to orgasm, you can fall asleep like this quite comfortably.

THE DRAWBACKS
Sex when you are practically asleep does mean that you tend not to use any kind of sex toy or aid, so any inadequacies in your technique will be more evident. And if one of you comes quickly, the tendency will be for him or her to fall asleep leaving their partner frustrated and perhaps, by now, wide awake. This is not a good way to finish the day, and can make for a problematic relationship if the situation is repeated.

There is also the problem of contraception. It's only too easy to let yourself get carried away when you

▲ *Being kissed and gently teased awake is a perfect start to the day.*

▼ *The spoons position is not too strenuous and allows the man to stimulate his partner's breasts and clitoris as they make love.*

are in that wonderfully drowsy state and completely forget to look for the condom or make the trip to the bathroom to insert the diaphragm. It's a good idea to make inserting a diaphragm, if you are likely to have sex, as much a part of your night-time routine as brushing your teeth, and condoms can always be kept as close as possible to the man's side of the bed – with a ready supply of tissues, of course! And remember that being sleepy is no excuse for fitting any contraceptive device sloppily.

One possible problem with having sex first thing in the morning, before you are properly awakened, is that one of you may be raring to go while the other might feel that sex is the last thing they want. A cup of coffee or a hot croissant maybe, but please, not sex, not just yet! Men's biological clocks dictate that they invariably wake up with an erection and a sparkle in their eye, and in most cases it is only natural to want to put it to good use. Women's libidos can vary enormously, so it is not uncommon for

men to start their day feeling wound up and frustrated.

As with almost anything else in a relationship, this can be dealt with by negotiation. You can make a deal that you owe your partner an orgasm – keep a tally if you want, although never let it get too serious – and promise him or her a really amazing session on, say, Saturday afternoon or

▲ *First thing in the morning is a very private and intimate time for couples, a great time for sex.*

▶ *Sleepy-time sex can be long and languorous or quick and frantic.*

Friday evening. But whatever else you do, keep your promise! There is an erotic menace surrounding the phrase 'I owe you an orgasm' – especially if whispered over the phone during office hours.

If you really do have trouble putting time aside for sex, even last thing at night, you ought to be looking at the whole of your relationship very seriously. Sex is an important part of loving, and to be too busy for it – ever – says a lot about the underlying problems and tensions in your relationship. When things start to go wrong it can happen that one of you goes to bed quite early and is – or pretends to be – fast asleep when the other one comes to bed, so sex is out of the question. It may be that you need to take a romantic break together, sort out problems with money or the kids, or that you need to have some counseling to help you over a rocky patch.

But sleepy-time sex is just as good as lovemaking at any other time if you both enjoy it and look forward to it. A good orgasm is the same no matter what the clock says. ❤

DOS AND DON'TS

DON'T FORGET THAT SEX FIRST THING IN THE MORNING MAY NOT BE YOUR PARTNER'S CUP OF TEA. IF THIS IS THE CASE, PUT SOME TIME ASIDE AT THE WEEKEND SO THAT YOU CAN INDULGE AT YOUR LEISURE.

DON'T FORGET TO USE CONTRACEPTION. WHEN YOU'RE FEELING SLEEPY FIRST THING IN THE MORNING OR LATE AT NIGHT, IT'S ALL TOO EASY TO FORGET TO GO TO THE BATHROOM TO FIND A CONDOM OR INSERT A DIAPHRAGM. IT'S A GOOD IDEA TO PREPARE IN ADVANCE FOR ANY EVENTUALITY!

DO MAKE TIME FOR SEX. IT'S AN IMPORTANT PART OF A RELATIONSHIP AND SHOULD NOT BE NEGLECTED. IF YOU FIND THAT YOU ARE ALWAYS TOO TIRED OR TOO BUSY FOR LOVEMAKING, PLAN A ROMANTIC WEEKEND AWAY WITH YOUR PARTNER.

INDEX

Index compiled by
INDEXING SPECIALISTS, Hove.